DISABILITY AND THE DISABLED-ISSUES, LAWS AND PROGRAMS

MENTAL HEALTH AND SOME SOCIOCULTURAL ISSUES IN DEAF PEOPLE

DISABILITY AND THE DISABLED-ISSUES, LAWS AND PROGRAMS

Additional books in this series can be found on Nova's website under the Series tab.

Additional e-books in this series can be found on Nova's website under the e-book tab.

PSYCHOLOGY RESEARCH PROGRESS

Additional books in this series can be found on Nova's website under the Series tab.

Additional e-books in this series can be found on Nova's website under the e-book tab.

DISABILITY AND THE DISABLED-ISSUES, LAWS AND PROGRAMS

MENTAL HEALTH AND SOME SOCIOCULTURAL ISSUES IN DEAF PEOPLE

BENITO DANIEL ESTRADA ARANDA

EDITOR

NOVA BIOMEDICAL

New York

For permission to use material from this book please contact us:
Telephone 631-231-7269; Fax 631-231-8175
Web Site: http://www.novapublishers.com

LIBRARY OF CONGRESS CATALOGING-IN-PUBLICATION DATA

Estrada Aranda, Benito Daniel.
Mental health and some sociocultural issues in deaf people / Benito Daniel Estrada Aranda.
p. cm.
Includes index.
ISBN 978-62948-577-5 (softcover)
1. Deaf--Mental health services. 2. Deafness--Social aspects. I. Title.
RC451.4.D4E85 2010
362.4'2--dc22 2010031164

Published by Nova Science Publishers, Inc. † New York

CONTENTS

Preface		**vii**
About the Authors		**ix**
Introduction	Purpose, Structure and Content of the Book *Benito Daniel Estrada Aranda*	**xiii**
Chapter 1	The Cultural Identity of Deaf People *Rosalinda Ruíz Ibarra*	**1**
Chapter 2	Abuse, Violence and Deaf Women *Lorena Ibarra and Nancy Muñoz Espinoza.*	**21**
Chapter 3	Sexuality of People with Deafness: Application of a Sex Education Program *Georgina Mitre Fajardo and Benito Estrada Aranda*	**51**
Chapter 4	Perceived Stress in Prelocutive Profoundly Deaf People *Benito Estrada Aranda, Mónica González Ramírez and René Landero Hernández*	**77**
Chapter 5	Profile and Intensity of Depression in Prelocutive Profoundly Deaf People in Mexico *Rosalinda Ruíz Ibarra and Benito Estrada Aranda*	**99**
Index		**117**

PREFACE

This book brings together a number of important issues within the area of mental health and deafness. The book is aimed at mental health professionals interested in learning more about the psychological reality of deaf people, and in particular, the course that takes two mental health disorders including, depression and stress. The psychological reality presented in this book also refers to other issues. Firstly, the issue of cultural identity and sexuality in other deaf people and the abuse and violence against deaf women and how this affects their social interactions.

ABOUT THE AUTHORS

Benito Estrada Aranda. He has a PhD and master's degree in Systemic Therapy form Pontifical University of Salamanca (Spain) and a degree in psychology from the Universidad Autonoma de San Luis Potosi (Mexico). He is a full-time research professor at the School of Psychology at the Universidad Autonoma de Nuevo Leon since 2006, member of the National System of Researchers (NRS) in the candidate level, PROMEP profile features and member of the Academic Board of Consolidated Social Psychology and Health in the research of psychosocial variables in health and family studies. He has published numerous scientific articles in refereed journals stringent international and index. He is also the author of several books and book chapters. He has directed bachelor thesis and master as well. He is currently involved in funded research and collaborative projects with academic leaders in Mexico and abroad. Email: bestrada@fap.uanl.mx

Georgina Mitre Fajardo. She has a Master's degree in habilitation and rehabilitation of persons with disabilities from the University of Salamanca (Spain) and a degree in psychology from the Universidad Autonoma de San Luis Potosí (Mexico). She is an independent researcher in the field of autism and is currently studying the quality doctorate at the University of Salamanca on "Advances in research and perspectives on disability." She has conducted research on deaf adolescents on sexuality and eye contact and imitation skills in children with autism. She is currently working on funded research and multidisciplinary collaborative projects with international researchers. Her current research is on communication skills in pre-linguistic children with autism. Email: gmitre@hotmail.com

Lorena Elizabeth Ibarra González. She has a BA in Psychology from the Universidad Autonoma de Nuevo Leon (Monterrey, Mexico), with a concentration in behavioral area. She has participated in workshops about pregnancy prevention and sexually transmitted infections in adolescents. She has worked as a therapist for deaf children and adolescents. She is collaborating on research projects such as the treatment of fibromyalgia and violence and abuse in deaf women. She is currently completing graduate studies in the Master of Science in Health Psychology at Universidad Autonoma de Nuevo Leon (Monterrey, Mexico) and CONACYT scholarship. Email: loreibarragzz@gmail.com

Mónica Teresa González Ramírez. She holds a PhD in Psychology from the National University of Distance Education (Spain). Master of science option in health psychology. Degree in Psychology from the Universidad Autonoma de Nuevo Leon (Monterrey, Mexico). She is a teacher and a full time researcher at the School of Psychology at the U.A.N.L. She is member of the National System of Researchers (SNI) at level 1, profile PROMEP and faculty member in Social Psychology (Consolidated), Faculty of Psychology Universidad Autonoma de Nuevo Leon. She has won two state awards for research, awarded by the State Ministry of Health in 2001 and 2002. She is the author of 23 papers published in international refereed journals, 10 book chapters and co-author of two books. She has worked as a teacher and researcher at the Autonomous University of Nuevo Leonfor the last seven years. The lines of research she develops is research methodology and psychosocial variables related to health and family studies, with emphasis on the study of stress. E-mail: monygzz77@yahoo.com

Nancy Lizeth Muñoz Espinosa. She holds a degree in psychology from the Universidad Autonoma de Nuevo Leon (Monterrey, Mexico), School of Psychology. During her undergraduate studies, she participated in the first training center to provide counseling services to deafwith deaf children mainly attending. Some of her experiences has been a teacher in preschool with children ages one to seven years.. She has worked in psychological counseling with families of deaf children and has taught several workshops at conferences aimed at both the deaf and their families listeners on topics such as sexuality, values, addictions, among others. She has participated in the development of educational work plans for deaf students, as well as an assistant teacher of Mexican sign language. She is currently working in the city of Monterrey in areas related to mental health. Email: nancita_2428@hotmail.com

René Landero Hernández. He has a PhD from the University of Nuevo Leon, Nuevo Leon, Mexico. He is a member of the National System of Researchers (SNI) at level 2, a member of the Mexican Academy of Sciences and leader of the Academic Board in Social Psychology (Consolidated), Faculty of Psychology at the University of Nuevo León. He has won two state awards for research, awarded by the State Ministry of Health. He is the author of 24 papers published in international refereed journals, 14 book chapters and author of three books. He has worked as a teacher and researcher at the Autonomous University of Nuevo Leon for over 20 years. The research lines are developed by research methodology and psychosocial variables related to health and family studies. E-mail: rlandero1_mx@yahoo.com.mx

Rosalinda Ruíz Ibarra. She holds a degree in psychology from the Universidad Autonoma de Nuevo Leon, School of Psychology. Her experience in the deaf community starts with the integration to the practice center with deaf people, where she learned Mexican sign language; she participated in the psychoeducational counseling of parents of deaf children and listeners. She has taught workshops for counseling deaf children, as a therapeutic intervention in the area of mental health. Close contact with the members of this community made her to know their social difficulties, which led her to develop her thesis work entitled "Intensity and profile of depressive symptoms in profound prelocutive deaf Mexicans." She currently works at the Instituto Tecnologico de Nogales (Nogales, Sonora) as Tutoring Program Coordinator.

Introduction

Purpose, Structure and Content of the Book

Benito Daniel Estrada Aranda

This book brings together a number of important issues within the area of mental health and deafness. Its creation has been a huge effort because this book was written by the project funded by the Ministry of Education under the program for the improvement of full-time faculty in institutions of public higher education in Mexico.

Some of the authors involved in this book were trainees of this project and worked on it for two years, derived from this effort and dedication thesis emerged with whom graduated in psychology. Other authors are full professors of the Faculty of Psychology at the Universidad Autonoma de Nuevo Leon, as the compilers of this book, are members of the National System of Researchers of the National Council for Science and Technology.

In this book we will write Deaf with "D" capitalized to refer to those people who born profoundly deaf or who lost his hearing before the first three years of life. This people also use sign language to communicate and identify with the deaf community and feel part of it. The book is aimed at mental health professionals interested in learning more about the psychological reality of eaf people, and in particular, the course that two mental health disorders take, including depression and stress. The psychological reality of which we speak also refers to other issues, such as cultural identity and sexuality in other eaf people and the abuse and violence against deaf women and how this affects their social interactions. The book is aimed at mental health professionals working with deaf patients, or who have contact with the deaf community and are interested in exploring the themes of the book, and disclosing information about these issues for deaf people in Mexico and Spain. Four of the five chapters of the book were written in Mexico and the one that addresses the issue of sexuality in the Deaf was written in Spain. This is a book that combines three chapters of research with two chapters of academic and theoretical review.

The reader can choose to read the chapters in the order that best fits their concerns and preferences, and hence provides a brief abstract of each one of them so you can design your route reading and can make a clear image of the contents of the book.

The first chapter is titled The Cultural Identity of Deaf people, prepared by Rosalinda Ruiz Ibarra and it analyzes the characteristics and implications of social and cultural identity in the deaf community. She defines social or cultural identity as part of the self that is constructed through the sense of belonging to a particular social group. In this chapter we consider that, in speaking of Deaf people, their identity is particularly influenced by cohesion and participation in the deaf community, or otherwise, for divorce and distance of the deaf world. To a large extent, this will determine the style that makes the individual identity. Each of these styles or stages of identity have their own positive and negative, that influences the individual's personal development, and in this chapter addresses each of these types of identity.

The second chapter is entitled Abuse, Violence and Deaf Women. It was written by Lorena Ibarra and Nancy Muñoz Espinosa with the aim of studying the history of this problem and analyze the current situation in a very complex, and unfortunately very present issue for deaf women. The contents of this chapter is divided into two parts, the first of which explores issues such as social inequality between women and men, theories about the circle of violence, common features have been observed in battered women, the differences between violence in women who are deaf and hearing, and why deaf women are a population of greater risk of violence, and finally, statistics are presented for estimating violence and the consequences it has on battered women. In the second part of chapter, one can find a review of treatment programs and psychotherapeutic techniques available to women victims of abuse and the difficulties due to lack of programs tailored to deaf women.

The third chapter is titled Sexuality of Deaf people. It was written by Georgina Fajardo and Benito Estrada Aranda. This chapter describes some models in the literature that represent the way in which they operate regularly with deaf people and partner relationships, as well as some factors that make a group more vulnerable to abuse, mistreatment and unwanted pregnancies. It also describes the process of implementing a sexual education program offered to a group of Deaf people in Spain, through which you can have a look at the real and current needs surrounding this population in the area of sexuality.

The fourth chapter is entitled Perceived Stress in Prelocutive Profoundly Deaf People in Mexico. It was written by Benito Estrada Aranda, Monica Gonzalez and Rene Landeros. In this chapter, the authors present an adaptation of a Perceived Stress Scale for Mexican sign language to assess stress in the profoundly prelocutive deaf population. This is a chapter of research which could let know that the perceived stress in deaf people in the sample is characterized by a greater perceived control of stressful stimuli but with a lower expression of these and other results.

The fifth and final chapter is entitled Intensity and Profile of Depression in Deaf People in Mexico. The chapter has been written by Rosalinda Ruiz Ibarra and Benito Estrada Aranda. A review of the record in the literature related to depression for deaf people, especially in the assessment methods used so far. Analyzes the profile and intensity of depressive symptoms in a sample of prelocutive profoundly deaf people in Mexico through the application of an instrument to measure the intensity of depressive symptoms across the Mexican sign language, and compares these results with similar data reported in Spain.

In summary, this book makes a valuable contribution to the scientific community interested in mental health and deafness as was done in a country (Mexico) where this line of research and work has been very poorly studied, thus there is few data available for the international scientific community on the psycho-social reality of deaf people in Mexico.

We hope that reading the chapters will be useful and pleasant for the reader and are practical in their various concerns, business needs, training and research.

Chapter 1

THE CULTURAL IDENTITY OF DEAF PEOPLE

Rosalinda Ruíz Ibarra

ABSTRACT

. This chapter discusses the characteristics and implications of social identity in deaf people. Social or cultural identity is a part of life that is constructed through the sense of belonging to a particular social group. Speaking specifically of deaf people, we find that their identity is particularly influenced by the cohesion and participation in the deaf community, or otherwise, for divorce and distance of the deaf world. Then the level of identification with deaf peers determines the identity style that makes the individual: listener, marginal, immersed, and bicultural. Each of these styles or stages of identity has its own positive and negative, that influences the individual's personal development, discussed in this chapter.

INTRODUCTION

In this chapter we review the theoretical and empirical contributions that have been presented on the issue of cultural identity of deaf people. Cultural identity is a phenomenon that has been studied in many other minorities, which is present in all individuals, as a characteristic of personality. Throughout the chapter we will discover the history of this construct and the way they have been developing theories that purport to explain.

Deaf identity has been prominent since the 1980´s. Its importance and empirical justification lies in finding out what kind of identity a deaf person may have, how they develop those types and what kind of deaf identity is more functional.

Largely deaf cultural identity is formed by a series of challenging stages by which it crosses (or remains) any deaf person trying to adapt to their condition of absence or hearing loss. Just like true personality traits, in the process of social construction of identity can be purchased desirable and undesirable traits, positive and negative, so the studies presented here help to know what those characteristics are in order to learn how to develop more positive social identity, as we do with personality traits.

In our country, the manifestation of deaf identity is present in the groups of deaf people who recognized themselves as a social, cultural and linguistic minority. As in the rest of the world, the mexican deaf community are known for cultural and idiosyncratic features well defined (Friedman, 1999b). However, despite the fact that Mexican Sign Language is recognized as an official language, surprisingly few scientific and political efforts have been made to promote equality of this community.

1. Theories of Social Identity

The word identity is defined by the Royal Academy of the Spanish Language as the "conscience that a person has to be itself and different from others." A person has a personal identity when he or she finds within themselves their own characteristics, that when compared with the people around them, make them different and unique. So in order to have a personal identity, it is necessary to know the set of values, beliefs, traits, behavior patterns and idiosyncrasies that distinguish us and make us different. Personal identity is therefore a set of features that are built over time, and that in our society is defined by the adolescent.

The process of identity is not fixed nor is oblivious to social interactions, but rather refreshes in social exchange and it is continuously fed from outside influence.

Humans, being social creatures by nature, seek to be accepted and belong to a group. Perhaps this search has been present in us from prehistory, where it was necessary to stay with the group to survive, because one man was unable to hunt, build a shelter, keep the fire, or doing any other activity requiring group collaboration.

Over the years we have studied this relationship between personal identity and sense of belonging to a certain social group and all the features involved. However, it is not until the early 1980's when this relationship is defined as cultural identity.

It was then that, if culture is the set of distinctive spiritual, material and emotional features of society or social group and encompasses, in addition to art and literature, lifestyles, fundamental rights human being, value systems, beliefs and traditions, then cultural identity would be part of our identity that we know belongs to a group and therefore distinguishes us from other individuals belonging to different groups.

Since the creation of urban communities, where individuals are increasingly divided in social groups, Tajfel and Turner (1986) developed the social identity theory (cultural) where intergroup behavior was integrated with the processes of single-motivational and cognitive-members of groups and social characteristics of the context in which the groups are interrelated. The work of Tajfel insists that both personal identity and individual behavior should be seen as parts of belonging to groups (Canto and Moral, 2005).

The membership also has a considerable influence on an individual's self-image. A part of the self-image is influenced by membership in different social categories, social identity is known. Tajfel (1984) proposed a comprehensive definition for this key phenomenon means that part of an individual's self-concept which derives from the knowledge of their social group membership, along with the evaluative and emotional meaning associated with that membership.

Therefore feeling part of a group influence each individual significantly, through three different processes (Tajfel and Turner, 1986):

a) Categorization: People tend to categorize objects to understand them, much like humans categorize people in this way to understand their social environment. These categories can be white, black, Australian, Christian, Muslim, etc., and function as a guidance system that creates and defines the place of the individual in society.
b) Identification: people identify with groups they believe they belong. The identification carries two meanings. Some of those who are governed by the group to which we belong, sometimes thought of as "us" and sometimes as "self." When we think of "us" cultural identity is defined.
c) Comparison: In some ways, we see ourselves as others, that is, we treat members of our group similarly. When it comes to assessing, we

> just compare ourselves with those members who belong to our group. And when we make comparisons to the outside as a group are "us" against "those."

The purpose of Tajfel and Turner (1986) to develop the Social Identity Theory was to explain the prejudice, discrimination and intergroup relations without resorting to personality factors of individuals or individual differences; trying not to reduce the collective phenomena of intra and interpersonal processes (Billig, 1976, Song and Moral 2005).

Within the collective phenomena which Tajfel refers, are minorities. These groups are composed of individuals who have in common some feature that makes them vulnerable to discrimination from the rest of society.

The study of minority groups and their social identity began in the late 1970s with the analysis of black identity development in African- Americans, culminating in the Theory of Minority Identity Development or minorities (MIDT) who studied groups of blacks, gays or feminists (Cross, 1971; Helms, 1990, Downing and Roush, 1985).

It is from these theoretical formulations that arise Theories of Development of Deaf Identity (Glickman, 1993; Holcomb, 1997, Maxwell and Zea, 1998) that attempt to explain the stages a person with hearing lossgoes through in order to identify with a social group (whether the group of deaf or group of listeners).

Although we deeply recognize the value of all the theoretical proposals on this issue, it is impossible to summarize them all in a single chapter. We will present in detail the proposed Glickman as being one that has a more solid empirical support, through the creation of the scale of the Deaf Identity Development (DIDS) and that statistical data portal underlying assumptions of his theory. Besides, the steps described by this author coincide in content with most published theories.

2. Theory of Deaf Identity Development

The theory of Deaf identity development, known as DIDT, was proposed by Glickman in 1993, and arises from the different theoretical proposals studying minority groups, especially the Theory of Development Minority Identity, because from his perspective, this theory provides a cognitive map that shows the process in which individuals become culturally distinct and a guide to how people construct their reality through different stages.

For Glickman three factors will determine the Deaf identity development:

1) The age of hearing loss. Knowing at what age hearing loss originated is a key factor that will allow us to place ourselves in the reality being faced by the deaf person. It is worthwhile to recognize that the earlier hearing loss occurs, the greater the impact on development in general and the psychosocial in particular. Of factors like this is that children grow up culturally deaf listeners, marginal or bicultural. According to the age at which shows will be divided into:

- Prelocutive deafness. In speaking of this type of deafness, we mean people who acquired it before the first three years of life, which means that have not yet acquired the spoken language. Because of this, prelocutive deaf children who do not know sign language (hereafter SL), will have significant delays in the area of education and social development.
- Postlocutive deafness. This type of hearing loss occurs when people have acquired the spoken language, that is, after three years. For them will be relatively easier to communicate, because they know the listener code.

2) Family type. Because 90% of deaf children are born into hearing families are not educated in deaf culture by their own families. The hearing parents of these deaf children also face the challenge of communication, to establish an emotional bond and from the communication containing the deaf child and provide a functional structure. Thus, in large measure, the impact on the cultural identity of the deaf child to acquire in the future, depends on the strategies that parents face with the child's deafness. For these and other reasons, the majority of deaf children are culturally marginal, even within their own families.

3) The language and communication. Communication in general, and especially through SL, is a significant emotional issue for deaf people. They, like many other social minorities, struggle to gain access to basic public services in their language. Bilingual education and medical care in sign language are examples of violations of fundamental rights of deaf people (Estrada, 2008). Deaf children of hearing families will face constant barriers to communication in general, and particularly in their family, which can have a profound impact on their psychological development and mental health.

The difference between deaf children who are born into a hearing family and children who are born deaf in a deaf family has, together with the above factors, a fundamental importance in the development of deaf identity.

2.1. Stages of Deaf Identity

According to MIDT, Glickman proposes four different stages or types of identity that can be found in a person with deafness:

A) Culturally Listener

It consists mainly of people who were deaf during or after adolescence. In these cases, generally, the personal and social identity is already defined, so that the individual identifies more with the group of listeners. For such people the hearing loss is usually due to serious illness, accident, or a gradual loss of hearing. All these reasons are unexpected, so the person who suffers is facing a condition of total ignorance of deafness and, of course, the deaf community.

In addition, the deaf person, suffers himself to be perceived as disabled and less competent than before. Luey and Per-Lee (1988 Glickman, 1993) describe the stages that people go through who are facing such a loss: shock, denial, anger, guilt, depression and adaptation. People who become deaf in adulthood, are usually pressured by their friends and family to speed through all these stages and come, with less damage, to the acceptance of their condition. But asking for an effort of this kind to a person who has lost his hearing is inconsistent when deafness is socially perceived as a terrible tragedy, a profound loss and a source of pain, grief and isolation.

Ignorance of what deafness is and what it means for members of the community, causes hearing people do everything possible to "re-enable" for deaf people (because they are disabled from their perspective), forcing them to use their residual hearing or oral communication resources.

For a culturally listener, these are all possibilities. They are unaware that there is sign language or special phones for the deaf or television programs tailored to their needs. And this ignorance t leaves them no choice but to be a deaf person who remains in the hearing world.

Cultural identity listener is a psychological reality for many people who lost their hearing in adulthood. Because the general population is listening and is familiar only with the characteristics of their own culture, including most teachers, doctors and mental health professionals working with this perspective listener, without submitting to their patients any choice. Of course the intention of all is creating a better quality of life for patients, from the perspective that "after all, the world is listening out there."

It is difficult for a hearing person to understand what it means to be a listener from the perspective of the deaf. The hearing person takes for granted that you can hear and see the impact of their condition. The deaf person can see the benefits that being most acute listener that the listener himself. For these reasons, it is difficult to describe precisely the characteristics of the cultural stage listener, because these features are part of the thinking of the general population.

What is important to understand is that a culturally deaf listener does not know the meaning of deafness to the deaf community, does not know the deaf culture as a group share, is disinterested in using alternative media (SL), are perceived themselves as disabled or less valuable and oral communication is used most of the time.

Glickman (1993) also notes the following features:

1. Deafness is defined as a medical disease and not as a cultural difference.
2. Medicine and technology must find ways to help deaf people to become members of society as capable listeners.
3. Hearing people are healthier than deaf people. People should strive to live as listeners and show it in their attitude, behavior, and way of perceiving the world, how to communicate, etc.
4. Deaf people are stereotyped as people with no social skills, isolated, less intelligent, etc. We must strive to be different from these stereotypes and stay away from contact with other deaf people.
5. One must strive to overcome barriers imposed by deafness. The successful deaf person is one that operates entirely in the hearing society without any support and without sign language.
6. A deaf person should seek professional listeners (counselors, teachers, audiologists, doctors, etc…) for advice and direction. These will be informed and benevolent.
7. Social policy and education are easier to ally with the oral. Using residual hearing, lip reading, spelling, is a positive value. Grouping deaf children in a classroom talks about "segregation" and expose them to a deaf adult is seen as a positive model as "pollution", because the children lose enthusiasm for joining the hearing society. Sign language is seen as a way to distort the language.

B) Culturally Marginal

As well as being culturally listener describes a stage of identity development relevant to the majority of deaf people who lose their hearing in adulthood, being culturally marginal becomes relevant to people who become deaf as children and are able to form a concept of what being a listener is, and define themselves as deaf with regard to this construct. This is the situation of most children born into deaf families.

Despite the efforts of families and teachers, children do not grow identified with hearing people. Education systems, oral and total communication in its various forms, are trying to instill listeners identities. What they really achieve is to create marginal identities, which should produce a bicultural identity.

Marginal identity may be the second step for people who have already been through the listener identity and begin to explore the world of the deaf. Or to the deaf children of deaf people, who have not been able to identify with the deaf community or with the listener.

Marginal identity also occurs when deaf children are born into hearing families and start feeling excluded by not being able to use oral language.

Culturally marginal people, by definition, have no well-established identity. They would rather stay in a state of confusion from the start, without having a clear view of which world they belong to. Marginal identity in children may manifest itself in psychological and behavioral problems, probably caused by the isolation suffered by not having the tools (SL) necessary to enable them to socialize and integrate.

People with marginal identity are on a thin rope that hangs between two groups, and usually they are present in different psychological traits: ambivalence, inferiority complex, hypersensitivity to perceive injustice, selfishness, aggression, among others (Stonequist, Glickman 1937, 1993).

The ambivalence experienced by people with marginal identity becomes clear when you come into contact with the two worlds. Hearing people are admired and imitated, but are secretly resentful and envious. Deaf people are, before others, neglected; however, the deaf are never more comfortable and happy with themselves, as when they're deaf.

Glickman summarizes the characteristics of this type of identity as it follows:

1. Few communication skills, both oral language (the language of their parents) and SL.

2. Inappropriate social behavior in both contexts (the listener and the deaf).
3. Difficulty in establishing and maintaining close relationships with either deaf or listeners. Besides a deep and abiding sense of isolation and bitterness.
4. Confusion about their identity.
5. Feeling of not belonging anywhere, caught between two worlds without finding a home.
6. Instability in relationships with both deaf and hearing people. Sometimes the deaf person is comfortable with other deaf people, sometimes hate being with them. Idolizes listeners that they envy
7. Marginal deaf generally used simultaneous communication (speaking and signs at the same time), plus sign on some variant of English (or language of your country) and not SL. Openly disapprove of the use of the SL to see it as an impediment to communication with listeners.

C) Culturally Immersed

The stage of immerse identity is characterized mainly by anger, especially towards the dominant group in society (the hearing), rejection of everything that belongs to this majority group, a passion fueled by everything pertaining to cultural minority (deaf), thinking dichotomous (you're one of them or you're one of us) and political movements.

Deaf people with immerse identity want to surround themselves with everything they believe is deaf, begin to classify the right and wrong way to be deaf and put labels of "mentality listener" to everything that does not fit with their view of the deaf. It's a stage of irrational people, who reject all deaf people who use their voices, sign in English, marry listeners or use hearing aids.

The position of immersion is more visible in areas traditionally more concerned with the deaf: the communication, the meaning of deafness, the interaction between deaf and hearing and control of the institutions for the deaf. Deaf people with immerse indentity expect that educational institutions are run by deaf. Deaf people believe should be educated, counseled and treated mainly, if not exclusively by the deaf.

The pathological view of deafness is strongly rejected. Instead, deafness is understood as a cultural difference rather than a disability. The complications that the condition of deafness can bring are seen as a result of hearing peoples control over them, and not as limitations of not listening.

It is believed with complete certainty that the appropriate language is the SL and totally rejects the oral language as the language of the oppressors. Use of oral language is unnecessary, even in listeners contexts , and is perceived as a violation of the rights and values of deaf.

The use of hearing aids (hearing aids, amplifiers, implants) is interpreted as a sign of listener oppression. Still others compare the use of cochlear implants or other surgical procedure to regain hearing with genocide (Harlan, 2005). The dominant feeling at this stage is anger, which is usually directed toward hearing people, however well intentioned they are.

To summarize, Glickman (1993) lists the following characteristics of the immerse identity:

1. Immersed in the deaf world. With an enthusiastic and uncritical view of everything that has to do with the deaf.
2. Idealization of the deaf world and rejection of the hearing world.
3. Tendency to think that deaf people can not do anything wrong, and listeners can not do anything right.
4. An inversion of listeners traditional values: the SL is superior to the language listener. Deaf people should never use their voices. Signer and talk at the same time is inappropriate. Only the deaf should be directing educational programs and counseling for the deaf.
5. General anger, but especially directed towards listeners.
6. The first part of this stage is characterized by being more "anti-listener" than "pro-deaf." Positive values of deaf people are defined by opposition to the values of the listeners, not what works to improve the quality of life of deaf people. In a second step the deaf begin to worry more about the welfare of their community, by alienating listeners.

D) Bicultural Identity

Bicultural identity is the final stage of the development of deaf identity. At this stage, the person reaffirms his deafness as a cultural difference and feels a deep connection with other deaf people. At the same time, the strengths and weaknesses of hearing and deaf people are recognized, thus promoting a balanced individual conceptualization of what it means to be deaf.

This stage may be the first for deaf children born into deaf families, as these have been in contact with the deaf culture and appropriate adult role models, have acquired at an appropriate age convenient mode of communication for them, and have learned to naturally interact with hearing persons from a bicultural perspective. All these advantages propitiate a superior academic and social performance to that deaf children who have hearing parents.

In fact, people who have been able to observe from within the deaf community, have realized that the leaders of this group are often deaf children of deaf parents, who have been educated under the influence of bicultural identity.

The main components of a bicultural identity should be:

1. Proud to be a deaf person, recognizing that both deaf and hearing have strengths and weaknesses
2. Possess adequate social skills to establish relationships with deaf and hearing without having a preference for either group. Comfortable in both worlds.
3. Show appreciation and respect for the spoken and the SL, recognizing them as two different languages that have the same value, and practice conversational skills that are kept for each language.
4. Having the ability to recognize and resist listener paternalism and any other form of oppression of the deaf world, maintaining friendly alliances with hearing persons that show an intention to cooperate selflessly.
5. A deep and personal view of what it means to be deaf.
6. The ability to appreciate and affirm the positive aspects of deaf culture.

Table 1. Abstract of the stages of deaf identity development (Glickman, 1993)

Stage	Reference group	Deafness interpretation	Deaf community interpretation	Expressed emotions
Hearing	Listener	Sickness	Ungroup an stereotyped	Depression and desperation
Marginal	Changing	Sickness	Changes between good and bad	Confusion and conflict
Immersion	Deaf	Cultural	Positive and no reflexive	Anger and "infatuation of deafness"
Bicultural	Deaf	Cultural	Positive, personal and integrative	Acceptance and proud to be a group

Glickman (1993) recognizes that these characteristics, and indeed the whole model of bicultural identity, requires a certain level of education and certain social interactions with the environment (both deaf and hearing). While in the United States is not difficult to achieve, in Mexico we are facing a truly dark reality for deaf people, as far as education, social acceptance and in respect for human rights (Estrada, 2008) refers .

It is important to remember that the process of establishing the identity is not static, so a person can spend several times by each of the stages before consolidated into one.

3. Cultural Identity in the Deaf Community

As we have seen, people who lose their hearing can pass through several stages before being defined as members of the silent community. Whether these experts classified into four stages (Glickman, 1993), seven (Holcomb, 1997) or a dichotomous scale (bicultural / acultural) that assesses five different dimensions (Maxwell and Zea, 1998), the ultimate goal is always the same: find the features that allow an individual to develop a healthy identity.

These same scholars of the deaf community have found that providing access to the community and deaf culture for people with hearing loss, so they can identify with a group, allows them to develop a healthy identity.

One of the reasons justifying the contact between deaf people refers to the need to organize their reality and their experiences in a way different from hearing people. Failing to hear an alarm (sirens, bells), not being able to interact with the hearing society, dominated by the oral-auditory language, not being able to use certain media (TV, radio) or not having access bilingual education, conditions the deaf to reorganize its reality. Sharing these experiences and this particular form of organizing their environment are some of the reasons why the deaf identify with each other, continually meet and form bonds and become a community (Domínguez, 2003).

This is the case with most contemporary of the deaf communities: a community cluster and eventually form a new kind of ethnic minority. Most deaf people in Mexico make up more than one ethnic minority , not only because they constitute a linguistic community, but because throughout its existence, as individuals and as a group relate to the world in a singular way (Fridman, 1999a).

So far, studies reveal that bicultural identity can lead to a more healthy personal development. But from the perspective of the deaf community's opinions seem to be in doubt. Carol Padden (1996), a recognized leader of the American deaf community, says that talking of being "bicultural" is not talking about a state of addition to one of the two cultures, rather it is to speak of states of tension to reconcile differences between both worlds. It is likely that such a state of permanent tension could lead to psychological problems. Despite this, the younger members of the deaf community are calling for parents to give them early access to the community, because in their point of view, this approach enables them to create a solid and healthy self-esteem and realistic expectations of hearing people and deaf (Holcomb, 1997). For these reasons, experts in the field such as Thomas Holcomb (1997), consider it essential that parents and educators of deaf children bring to them to the community and deaf culture, so they can develop positive reactions toward their condition of deafness, and therefore a bicultural identity that allows them to establish healthy relationships with both deaf and hearing listeners.

4. Manifestations of Cultural Identity

Deaf cultural identity is manifested in daily life as in any other culture. For Carol Padden and Tom Humphries (1984) cultural events that characterize the group of deaf people are:

- Language. The deaf community has a common language, Sign Language. The use of gesture-spatial language has references since ancient times, until 1620 when Juan Pablo Bonet published his 'Reduction of Letters and Art to teach the mute to speak', explicitly using sign language as a form of communication for the deaf. However, the SL is not a universal language, every country has its own sign language, creating an interesting integration of the deaf culture and national identity (Cruz, 2008).
- History. Deaf people, like any other social minority, share among themselves a history, which in many cases is related to the oppression and discrimination. This story includes the major international leaders; deaf people who have excelled despite their condition and who have made public the oppression of their community. Among them are teachers like Laurent Clerc, Helen Keller, great scientists like Thomas Edison, artists such as Francisco Goya, Marlene Matlin, among many others (Carroll and Mather, 1997). The story also includes the struggle for social equality, the creation of specialized

schools and higher education, the right to bilingual education and the recognition of their language, access to health services and employment opportunities. And of course the story also is full of traditions and customs.

- Experiences in common with hearing people. These experiences can be both positive and negative experiences. The results of the interaction between deaf and hearing depends on two factors: the stage of identity being experienced by the deaf person and ideology and perception of deafness by the hearing person.
- Strong social networks. The creation of social support networks is a feature that is present in almost all minority groups. Coexisting with people who are familiar with your condition makes you feel understood and supported, no one can understand the situation of a deaf as a deaf, and this causes deaf people to feel comfortable with each other and free to express their feelings. Probably because of thiswithin the community, all kinds of activities are promoted, such as recreational, educational and social, including deaf marriages, which are very common.

To Boris Fridman (1999), a Mexican linguistic expert and one of the main supporters of the deaf community in the fight to defend their right to official recognition of their language, expressions of deaf identity occur in everyday details, which can be crossed banal. However, Fridman says himself (1999a), "all of life is a network of trivialities." Among this series of everyday details it may be found the following details:

1. For the deaf, the dark means silence. For a couple of listeners, a dinner by candlelight is the representation of romance;or the deaf it is a moment of embarrassment and silence.
2. Eye contact is a priority. For example, the deaf can interpret placing a centerpiece as a sign of contempt or lack of cordiality to prevent eye contact
3. Gossip. Although it may seem strange, gossip is almost a ritual within the deaf community in general, and Mexico in particular. According to Boris (1999), gossip is a normal reaction by the silent community After all, they can not hear the news from radio or television, the press is not an option for the deaf in our country who hardly have access to a decent and bilingual education. For these reasons, they all hope anyone with some information to share it.

4. The groups and associations. Young people and adults, often gather in groups and associations, although they are a great way to enrich their intellect and personality, are not free of problems, frictions and misunderstandings, especially when two leaders (innate) have opposing views, which can lead to dissolve the group.
5. Marriage. Marriage between members of this community is extremely common, after all, within the group is where relationships develop more intimate and empathetic.
6. The deaf community in our country and the world, is constantly being renewed and transformed. This is because children of what now comprise the group of deaf, 95% of cases will be listeners. The new deaf therefore, are those who are not familiar with deaf culture and met one by chance or at school.
7. The deaf do not share their identity with their relatives. Unlike other ethnic groups, the deaf do not share their membership to the silent community with their family.
8. The hard of hearing seeking an advantage. Because hearing people feel more comfortable communicating with a hearing impaired person than with a profoundly deaf person, the former tend to take this advantage to play a mediating role between the two worlds, pretending to be seen as the leader of the group.
9. The hearing impaired is one who denies his deaf identity. Deaf people tend to view with suspicion those having hearing loss still behave as listeners, trying to speak. The sign of hearing impaired can be used either as people with residual hearing as in profoundly deaf and usually denote who is assumed not to be deaf and tries to live as a listener.

In her study with the deaf, Venezuelan Maria Eugenia Dominguez (2003) details one more of the daily differences between the deaf culture and the listener. This is a complimentary custom conflict between listeners and deaf listeners (teachers in the particular case of study) often complain of "bad manners" of the deaf (students in this case), who get through space of dialogue among listeners without "permission." After a series of detailed analysis, the study takes the view that cultural differences are responsible for the apparent rudeness of the deaf. Deaf people who "cross communication" of two listeners, if they make a gesture of cordiality that seeks to reconcile or excuse the interrupted with who interrupts: they accelerate the march, shrug their shoulders, down their chin and avoid eye contact. All with the goal not to impede communication between the two people who are communicating, as a gesture of empathy and warmth that is not perceived by listeners.

5. Implications of Cultural Identity in the Deaf Community

5.1. Results of Empirical Research

As we have reviewed so far, the cultural identity that deaf people may have could have a major influence in all areas of their life. Scientific research that has been conducted on this issue, pretends to know what is the healthiest kind of identity.

The results seem to agree with the idea that the environment in which operates a deaf person, it makes more favorable the risk of mental disorder. But if this environment is full of opportunities for interaction on its channel of communication, deaf children and adults have less risk of these disorders. Denmark (1994) states that "in general, how to manifest mental disorders in the deaf community, depends on a wide number of factors such as intelligence, personality, previous history, communication method and type of disorder".

As a clear example of the effects that the environment can have on the psychological development of deaf people, there is the work of Glickman (Black and Glickman, 2006; Glickman, 2007) performed in a psychological specialized care clinic for people with hearing loss. In them, Glickman has found that those who have a higher rate of psychological problems are those who have not been able to develop adequate competition in the language (whether oral or SL lenguage) and therefore do not have a strong identity.

Other studies of cultural identity, such as Yael Bat-Chava (2000), found that people who have a deaf and bicultural identity have higher scores on self-esteem; this is, people that accept their deafness and are provided by people who accept them equally, develop higher self-esteem than those who are deaf, who are not immersed in the deaf community, or the listener. And generally, the more severe the hearing damage, the greater the influence of this on the development of deaf identity (Colangelo and McWhirter, 2001), and there will be a greater identification with other deaf.

Supporting these findings are studies such as Cornel and Lyness (2004), who found that individuals with bicultural identity have higher self-esteem, and therefore lower risk of some kind of psychological disorder, in contrast to individuals with an identity marginal, who report lower scores on self-esteem and increased risk for eating disorder symptoms (Moradi and Rottenstein, 2007). The results of Leigh and Anthony (1999) also indicate that depressive symptoms are lower in deep deaf than hard of hearing, coinciding with the idea that the more deep the hearing loss, the greater their identification with the deaf community.

After all, it appears that the limitation in the communication is a factor that can lead to social and psychological disorders, as well as individual behavior patterns (Hyndley, 2000). On the other hand, the limitation on communication, is more prevalent in families of deaf children with hearing parents, than in families of deaf children with deaf parents, since in the latter the children develop a deep identification with the deaf community because they have had the opportunity to grow in the deaf culture and to use the SL.

CONCLUSIONS

Throughout this brief chapter, we tried to summarize the different kinds of identity, their characteristics, manifestations and implications. After analyzing the concept of cultural identity, it is clear that although hearing loss is due to a disease, its implications are given more weight in the psychological and social area than the medical. Before all these studies that considers and notes the existence of a distinct social group with its own characteristics, deafness could be seen from a pathological view where language specialists and speech therapy were the only ones able to save from disgrace those unfortunate enough to have this hearing impairment.

We can now see how, through different countries on all continents, the socio-cultural and anthropological prevails: it conceives "the deaf subject not as a sufferer but as a subject with cultural and anthropological aspects arising from their status as deaf, the most important of them: the need to use a visual language, that is, a sign language" (Domínguez, 2003).

However, despite the fact that currently the concept of deafness starts to heal, much remains to be done in this area. It is necessary to recognize the silent community their fundamental rights, beginning with disclosing their language, with particular emphasis on syntactic and semantic complexity that SL has, leaving behind the idea that sign language is like doing mime or learning a few signs.

In our country, under the policy of integration, the deaf children complete basic education in most cases, unable to read and write and above all, without access to bilingual models that help them develop a healthy cultural identity.

We must support the creation of autonomous educational institutions where students get truly quality education through deaf teachers, because these are the true models of bicultural identity.

Currently the Mexican deaf community has struggled to forge their own social identity, often in spite of their families,and must receive the support of their group to overcome the alienating environment of parents and siblings who are not worthy and don`t have effective communication with them. Deaf Mexicans today recall with sadness the days when the future looked promising for the community, through the efforts of the federal government itself with the creation of the National School of the Deaf. But in their memory is also the disappointment and disillusionment lived when the school was closed and they were forced to live marginalized and subjected to oral language. The deaf have lived alongside indigenous groups, ethnocide and have known and will continue in the process of developing resistance and fight for their cause, all under the protection provided by their own community.

References

Bat-Chava, Y. (2000). Diversity of deaf identities. *American annals of the deaf, 145*(5).

Black, A., and Glickman, N. (2006). Demographics, psychiatric diagnoses, and other characteristics of North American deaf and hard of hearing inpatients. *Journal of deaf studies and deaf education, 11:3.*

Canto, O. and Moral, T. (2005). El sí mismo desde la teoría de la identidad social. *Escritos de psicología*, vol.7.

Carroll, C. and Mather, S. (1997). *Movers and Shakers: Deaf people who changed the world.* California: Dawn Sign Press.

Colangelo, L., and McWhirter, J. (2001). The deaf identity development scale; a revision and validation. *Journal of counseling psychology*, 48(3).

Cornell, S., and Lyness, K. (2004). Therapeutic implications for adolescent deaf identity and self concept. *Journal of feminist family therapy, 16*(3).

Cross, W. (1971). The Negro-to-black conversion experience. *Black World,* vol.20: 13-25.

Cruz, A. (2008). La educación del sordo en un modelo bilingüe intercultural. *Ethos Educativo*, 41, pag 181-192. Obtenido el 22 de julio de 2009 en http://www.imced.edu.mx/EthosWeb/Archivo/41-181.pdf.

Denmark, J. (1994). *Deafness and Mental Health*. Pennylvania: J. Kingsley Publisher.

Domínguez, M. (2003). Pide permiso, maleducado: Sobre una diferencia de cortesía entre sordos y oyentes venezolanos. *EDUCERE: Articulos Arbitrados*, Vol 6(21), pag 19-25.

Downing, N. and Roush, K. (1985). From passive-acceptance to active commitment: A model of feminist identity development for women. *The counseling Psychologist*, 13(4), 695-709.

Estrada, A. B. (2008). La vulneración de los derechos humanos de las personas Sordas en México. *Revista del Centro Nacional de Derechos Humanos*, 3, (8), pp. 105-127.

Fridman, M. (1999a). La comunidad silente de México. *Viento Sur, 14.*

Fridman, M. (1999b). La realidad bicultural de sordos e hispanohablantes. Obtenido el 20 de Julio de 2009 en http://www.consejopromotor.org.mx/educacion/ponencias/1PROBL-1/M9_53B~1.html.

Glickman, N. (1993). *Deaf Identity Development: Construction and Validation of a Theoretical Model.* Tesis de doctorado no publicada, Universidad de Massachusetts.

Glickman, N. (2007). Do you hear voices? Problems in assessment of mental status in deaf persons with severe language deprivation. *Journal of deaf studies and deaf education, 12:2.*

Harlan, L. (2005). Ethnicity, Ethics, and the Deaf-World. *Journal of Deaf Studies and Deaf Education, 10:3.*

Helms, J. (1990) *Black and White racial identity: Theory, research and practice*. Wesport, CT: Greenwood Press.

Hindley, P. (2000). Child and adolescent psychiatry. En P. Hindley and N. Kitson (Eds.) *Mental Health and deafness,* (pp. 42-74). Londres: Whurr Publisher.

Holcomb, T. (1997). Development of Deaf Bicultural Identity. *American Annals os the Deaf*, vol. 142:2, pg.89.

Leigh, I., and Anthony, S. (1999) Parent bonding in clinically depressed deaf and hard of hearing adults. *Journal of Deaf Studies and Deaf Education, 4(1),* p.28.

Maxwell, D., and Zea, M.C. (1998). The Deaf Acculturation Scale (DAS): Development, reliability, and validity. Poster session presented at the

106th Annual Convention of the American Psychological Association. San Francisco, CA.

Moradi, B., Rottenstein, A. (2007). Objectification theory and deaf cultural identity attitudes: roles in deaf women`s eating disorder symptomatology. *Journal of counseling psychology, 54*(2).

Padden, C. (1996). From the cultural to the bicultural: The modern deaf community. En Ila Parasnis (Ed.), *Cultural and language diversity and the deaf experience*. New York: Cambridge University Press.

Padden, C. and Humphries, T. (1984). *Deaf in America: Voices from a culture.* Cambridge, MA: Harvad University Press.

Tajfel, H. (1984). *Grupos humanos y categorías sociales*. Estudios de Psicología Social. Barcelona: Editorial Hender.

Tajfel, H. and Turner, J. (1986). *The Social Identity Theory of Intergroup Behavior.* 2nd editin. Chicago: Nelson-Hall.

Trujillo, G. (2004). Identidad social Alemana a catorce años de la reunificación. Tesis de licenciatura no publicada, Universidad de las Américas Puebla.

Chapter 2

ABUSE, VIOLENCE AND DEAF WOMEN

Lorena Ibarra and Nancy Muñoz Espinoza

ABSTRACT

This chapter is intended to make an exploration of violence and abuse to deaf women. The importance of this issue is that gender-based violence currently reports alarming statistics. The National Institute of Public Health reports that 2 out of 3 women have experienced violence at some time in their lives. The chapter is divided into various sub-themes that examine issues such as: social inequality between women and men; theories about how the cycle of violence is maintained, some common features in battered women, the differences between violence in deaf women and listener women, and why a group of deaf women are at greater risk: estimation statistics of violence against women; consequences of violence in battered women, and finally treatment programs and psychotherapeutic techniques available to battered women and their difficulty by the lack of adaptation to deaf women.

INTRODUCTION

This chapter is intended to make an exploration of abuse against deaf women. Domestic abuse is an issue that, over time, has consistently attracted more attention; currently is not uncommon to see reports about it on the internet, television, newspaper and other media. In this connection, the

National Institute of Public Health reported alarming numbers: one out of five women suffer violence from their current partner, and two out of three women have experienced violence at some time in their lives. For many it is believed that violence against women has been increasing over the years, but now more cases are known and there have been more complaints against male aggressors. The origin of violence against women is usually due to the way how society is organized. In Mexico, we still live in a sexist, and mostly traditional society, which gives greater importance to man while the woman is lagging as belonging to the weaker sex. This results in men feeling they have power over women. And the violence and abuse are used by the aggressors as a quick way to solve problems or to "put women in their place."

The contents of this chapter is classified into two parts: the first is divided into sections that explore issues such as social inequality between women and men; theories about the cycle of violence, common features have been observed in battered women , the differences between violence in women who are deaf and hearing, and why deaf women are a population at higher risk, an estimation of statistics of violence and the impact it has on battered women. The second part of the chapter consists of treatment programs and psychotherapeutic techniques available to women victims of abuse and the difficulties encountered due to the lack of programs tailored to deaf women.

1. Inequality and Violence between Women and Men

To begin this section we would like to mention as background that the World Conference on Women in Beijing in 1995 recognized the importance of changing the focus of violence in women to gender violence, pointing to the eradication of violence as necessary first to eliminate the unequal society. Referring to this, we want to make a difference between gender and sex. Sex refers to a biological concept, people have different sex, for example, male and female. Gender is a social concept, as are the characteristics that society attributes to people depending on their sex. The importance of differentiating between these two terms is because for a long time it was believed that gender is inherent to biological differences. Following this idea, it is believed that men are made to be emotionally stable, have self-control, be aggressive, dominant, rational and courageous; while women are made to be passive, submissive, dependent, emotional and intuitive. However, the differences listed have little to do with sex, it's just gender; differential socialization to which we are exposed depending on whether we are women or men. Therefore, male domination is not a biological fact, but is a product of the education we receive and gender roles that we awarded (Mun Man Shum, Conde, and Portillo, 2006). Given this, how does gender relate to violence towards deaf women? As mentioned earlier, we mistakenly believe that men are naturally aggressive and dominant. This belief results in society legitimizes violence as natural and man be acquitted of responsibility.

Another reason to focus on eradicating gender violence is that it does not happen by itself, but occurs within a context. It is within the family where they began to teach gender stereotypes, by the expectations of mothers and fathers to the behavior of their children, and different ways of dealing with children depending on gender and the unequal relations between mother and father. Most families today are still traditional, meaning that work hierarchically, leading inevitably to a relationship of power between men and women who make that individuals are positioned asymmetrically. Usually the father is the head of household and who exercises authority, while the mother is responsible for the care of the house and children. Thus, the children begin to internalize the values, expectations and differentiated roles for men and women. However, not only in the family takes place this gender socialization, it happens in schools, in the religious sphere, in the media and even the social value, in this way are being created stereotypes.

In the case of deaf woman, a woman stereotyping discrimination is added by having a disability. Thus, deaf women are more exposed to various forms of violence as compared with women listeners, have greater dependence on their partner, child abuse awareness and lower levels of schooling. We will explain these differences in greater detail in the section, Differences Between dDeaf and Hearing women.

When we speak of the violence exercised by men against women, we refer not only to physical or sexual violence, which are the most observable. Currently there is a context of change in some areas of society, where the explicit violence against women is no longer remarkable, or presumption. However, there are still implicit forms of socially acceptable violence and abuse that are manifested in ordinary language, in nonverbal behaviors and various manifestations of power. For example, it is considered as a manifestation of excessive protection to the part of men to women, the insinuations, the insults, racist expressions, among others, but generally society does not consider itself as violence.

We also believe it is important to differentiate between the causes of violence against women and the factors that reinforce it. Usually mentioned as causes are alcohol or drugs, stress, unemployment, among others These are factors that sometimes accompany and accentuate the violence, but are not the reasons that cause violence against women. Violence against women is explained by the fear of some men to lose their identity and dominance in the patriarchal system, even in the household, and whether or not they are fully aware of how they use that power, it is an assault on the rights of women to be autonomous and a sample of the inability of many men to live together with different women. The offender man sees the woman as an object belonging to him, so he is jealous, possessive and controlling towards her and when a woman decides to act differently to their gender role, the man feels that she is not obeying his will, he feels humiliated and resorts to violence.

The importance of early awareness on violence against women lies in the possibility that abuse increases as time passes. Battered women often report that 90% of cases of violence began with a slap, but the beatings and assaults continued over time, more and more often and with more serious consequences (Mun Man Shum, Conde, and Portillo, 2006). Similarly, psychological or emotional violence may be only a preamble to the physical or sexual abuse.

Making aware of the various types of violence exercised by men against women, both socially acceptable behavior and not, and the way in how they develop within society, is essential to implement strategies of intervention. Similarly, we believe that attention should be paid to the male perpetrators, especially in the case of violence against deaf women, and women who are part of the deaf community who are often associated exclusively with other deaf people, and the few investigations of violent deaf men and rehabilitation programs available and adapted to them.

2. Theory of the Cycle of Violence

In this section we explain two theories about the cycle of violence, initially proposed by Walker (1979) and Deschner (1984).

According to Walker (1979), the abuse takes place in three phases, taking into account the emergence of the first episode of abuse and the first cycle of violence increases the likelihood of further episodes. These episodes will be taking place for even smaller situations and accompanied by more serious abuse. The phases are:

1. Accumulation Phase or Building of Tension

The tension arises over everyday conflicts. The offender abuses verbally and psychologically, sometimes causing minor injuries, usually deny the occurrence of the episode. The battered woman believes to have some control over the frequency and severity of abuse and tries to avoid increasing it using some strategies (reassuring the aggressor, avoiding certain behaviors, being passive, blaming herself). Women experience confusion and anxiety, and may try to get away from the aggressor. This makes the aggressor increase control over her.

2. Phase of Aggression or Discharge of Tension

Increase the intensity of the abusive episodes and appears in both physical and psychological abuse and / or sexual. The discharge of aggression alleviates tension of the abuser. The woman again implements the first phase strategies for survival and to stop the abuse. Usually at this time is when women report the abuse they suffer.

3. Phase of Repentance, Reconciliation or Honeymoon

The offender is repentant and assures the situation will not happen again. This behavior is positive reinforcement for women, and allows them to see the positive side of the relationship and fosters hope and desire that the offender will change. If a woman threatens to leave the abuser, he can get to pledge or do almost anything to get her back. If the relationship moves forward, it does so with a tension that would cause the back to the first phase.

Later, Deschner (1984) proposed a more specific model of the cycle of violence:

1. *Mutual dependence.* The beginning is a relationship between two people who feel a strong need for each other. It is a high-intensity emotional bond where both take vows of devotion to exclude other relationships and the outside world.
2 *Problematic event.* The victim does something that the aggressor perceives as undesirable, this may be something completely trivial. The situation gets out of the contract of mutual dependence. The attacker feels abandoned and rejected, but due to lack of communication of feelings, this is not communicated to the partner.

3. *Exchange of co-actions.* The attacker tries to stop the undesirable situation, usually through verbal threats, the other partner responds to threats. The anxiety of the situation will increase.
4. *Last resource.* The attacker sees the situation as unsustainable, there appears to be reached out to the point. This decision is key, certain cultural norms affect the speed with which it reaches this point.
5. *Primitive fury.* The attack comes as a result of the previous decision. The aggressor attacks household items, the couple or the children, who are beaten even more than necessary to win. The attacker is flooded with anger and rational mind disappears, he even forgets what was done during the attack.
6. *Reinforcement of aggression and instigation of fear.* During the attack, the victim ceases her behavior as a way to survive the attack and not to provoke more anger. With this, the victim is sending the message that violence stops what bothers the aggressor. If the victim was not seriously injured, she can try to calm the aggressor with gestures that indicate submission (blame herself for what happened, being more helpful). Once the attack occurs, the fear becomes an active ingredient in the relationship.
7 *Repentance phase.* The attacker, due to its partial amnesia, can hardly believe the magnitude of his violence and promises not to do it again. The victim sees repentance as really honest and gives one more chance to the attacker, despite their feelings of fear and anger. Unfortunately, the submission during the previous phase has reinforced the emergence of new violence. With each repetition of the cycle, increases the fear and the repentance phase becomes less convincing.

3. Characteristics of Abused Women

In relation to the profile of abused women, is reported in previous literature that factors such as income, education level, to be or not to be a housewife, passivity, hostility, self-esteem, alcohol intake, type of work, lifestyle or personality are not consistently associated with being a victim of abuse (Walker, 1999, Garcia-Moreno, 2000). Previously it was thought that battered women were of lower classes, uneducated, unemployed and belonged to minority groups in society. However, this profile was because battered women of lower classes and minority groups needed to use public resources and they could be easily noticed, while women with greater economic resources could better hide their abuse. According to Garcia-Moreno (2000) and Walker (2009), the most powerful single risk indicator to be abused is simply being a woman.

Other common ideas about battered women is that they are masochistic and emotionally dependent, and they support the violence of the aggressors in an average of 5-10 years, often from the engagement or the first year of marriage (Echeburúa E., Corral, Sarasua, and Zubizarreta, 1996). However, the violent relationship is maintained by various factors (Zubizarreta, Sarasua, Echeburúa, Corral, Sauce, and Emperor, 1994; Pagelow, 1997; Heise, Ellsberg, and Gottemoeller, 1999; Vázquez, 1999; Kelly, 2000), among these may include:

a) *Characteristics of abuse.* The longer the duration and severity of abuse, the less likely they are to leave the relationship because of fear, dependency, guilt and low self-esteem.
b) *Material and social resources available.* The economic dependence, lack of resources, lack of external support and social embarrassment make it difficult to abandon the relationship.
c) *History of abuse in women.* Exposure to maltreatment in the family during childhood may cause women to consider violence as normal and get used to enduring it
d) *Traditional attitudes.* The attitudes and beliefs about the man being superior make women see the abuse of his partner as justifiable.
e) *Ability to assume the end of the relationship.* When a woman leaves a violent relationship,she is gradually resuming control over their lives but in doing so, is also taking the failure by being wrong in choosing a mate and that could be seen as a blow to her self-confidence. The decision to abandon the offender has been found to depend on the age of women, their cultural level, the existence of a job outside the home and social support.
f) *Fear.* Although the woman is ready to end the violent relationship, there is a possibility that the man aggressor refuses to lose control of the situation and decide to harass, persecute or even kill .

Coupled with the above factors, there are features specifically for women with disabilities that affect the decision to leave the violent relationship or stay in it, for example, greater dependence, perceiving herself as weak or vulnerable, the risk of being manipulated by others, lack of information about their rights, feelings of helplessness, stereotyped perception of being less as a person, inability to recognize abuse, among others (Brodwin and Siu, 2007).

We will mention two theories that have served to explain why women find it difficult to escape an abusive relationship and decide to stay with their abusers: the theory of battered woman syndrome and the theory of the survivor.

The first theory was adapted by Lenore Walker on the theory of learned helplessness by Seligman (1975). Walker used the term battered woman syndrome to see a pattern of signs and symptoms that occurred after a woman had been abused physically, sexually and / or psychologically in an intimate relationship when the partner exercised power and control over her. This syndrome consists of two defined elements : the cycle of violence (described above) and learned helplessness described by Seligman in laboratory animals.

The learned hopelessness theory predicts that the ability to perceive that one is able to control what happens may be damaged, this is because of the contingency loss, between response and consequence. Walker says that in the field of domestic violence, sporadic brutality, feelings of powerlessness, lack of financial resources and superior force of the aggressor, combine to instill a sense of hopelessness in the victim. The term hopelessness caused confusion at first because it made to see battered women as passive, but Walker pointed out that there comes a time when the victims do not try to stop the abuse, but they develop coping strategies to live with the possibility of continuing to be abused. What is lost in the learned hopelessness is motivation to keep trying to escape the violence.

Walker's research (2009) have shown that battered woman syndrome has six sets of criteria that identify it. These are:

1. Intrusive memories about the traumatic event.
2. High levels of anxiety.
3. Avoidant behaviors and emotional numbness usually expressed as depression, dissociation, minimization, repression and denial.
4. Harmful or dysfunctional interpersonal relationships, the product of the aggressors power and control.
5. Distortion of body image and / or somatic or physical complaints.
6. Difficulties in sexual intimacy.

The theory of battered woman syndrome provided a coherent and reasonable explanation to the prevailing theory at the time, which was that women somehow felt to deserve the abuse, that they were masochistic or had personality traits that caused the provocation of the aggressor (Shainess, 1979).

The second theory to be mentioned is the survivor one, proposed by (Gondolf and Fisher, 1988) in his book, Battered Women as Survivors: An Alternative to Treating Learned Hopelessness. In this, the authors criticize the model of learned hopelessness and refer to statistics that refute it. They report that battered women in their sample persistently sought help from different sources, and the more prolonged and intense the abuse, the greater was the variety and scope of their search for outside help.

In short, the theory assumes that surviving a pattern of abuse causes the battered woman to use innovative coping strategies, such as flattering the abuser and seeking help from family. When sources become ineffective assistance, battered women seek other resources and use different strategies to reduce abuse, how to avoid the abuser or seek legal help.

However,when a battered woman seeks foreign aid, often meets with little social support, ineffective bureaucracy and insufficient support resources, especially in the case of a disabled woman. Therefore, Gondolf and Fisher suggest that it is not learned hopelessness but the lack of options, combined with the lack of financial resources of the victim that infuse a feeling of anxiety that prevent them from escaping abuse and keep trying to change the aggressor.

The survivor theory emphasizes coping and survival skills of battered women, and suggests that cognitive motivational and behavioral deficits are found in individuals and agencies that fail to respond adequately to the request for assistance.

4. Differences between Women's Violence in Deaf and Hearing

As mentioned in previous sections, deaf women are at greater risk of violence and abuse due to a double discrimination: on the one side are the stereotypes of women, and this is compounded by her being deaf. This implies that even within the deaf community. women suffer more discrimination than deaf men. However, discrimination is not only happening in the deaf community, but also in the hearing world.

Here are a number of subtopics that explain the differences between deaf women and women listeners, leading to an increased risk of abuse and number of abuses in women with disabilities.

Deaf Men and Deaf Women

The reasons for deaf women to be at a disadvantage compared to men who are deaf are diverse. Among them are the overprotection for women with disabilities, which happens from the family environment and creates greater dependence; low self-esteem because of prejudice about disability and gender stereotypes and roles (in this case; female, for example: beauty, maternity) that are evaluated more negatively on women with disabilities than men, and little social contact outside the deaf community.

Family

It is common for families with a disabled daughter to create an atmosphere of overprotection, treating her differently than the rest of the family members, rarely giving them tasks or responsibilities and seeing themas victims. The over-familiar and shame, far from being considered, is just a manifestation and otherwise hinders the chances of women with disabilities to deal and see relations as equal, resulting in a lower degree of autonomy, making decisions and low self-esteem.

It is very important to create positive relationships in families with daughters who are deaf, because this depends on self-acceptance and the future of the deaf person.

The way in which the family deasl with their daughter's disability will affect psychosocially in deaf adult women (Iniesta, 2004), therefore, if deafness is viewed from a negative standpoint and disabling, deaf girls will internalize negative messages about their own condition and subjective limitations will be created as to their potential.

Similarly, due to overprotection and little social contact outside the family, women with disabilities are vulnerable to violence. This vulnerability is due to the family because the deaf women are treated as unable to do tasks, lack of intelligence or unable to make decisions by themselves, so they are constantly around to continue helping in their daily lives. Over time, this lifestyle ibecomes acceptable to other members of the family and the deaf woman (Torices, 2003).

A serious family difficulty that deaf women face is that the family rarely uses sign language as a means of communication, and instead, it tends to bind the deaf woman to use spoken language. For example, a deaf woman in the study of Mun Man Shum, Conde y Portillo (2006) comments:

> "I wish my mother was deaf, hopefully, we would have no problems, we would be hours and hours and hours recovering the time she should. [...] Yes, yes, because no communication from tiny many years. [...] Now she lets me, but during a season she didn´t allow me with hands, no hands that is terrible, not your hands which is really bad, and me with my mouth, you imagine, because she did not accept what happened"(p. 133)."

Currently, the General Law of Persons with Disabilities (House of Representatives, 2005) recognizes the Mexican Sign Language (MSL) as part of the linguistic heritage of the deaf community in Mexico. However, only few hearing families use SL to communicate with their deaf daughters or sons, whether due to a refusal to learn the language, not to accept her daughter's deafness, a fear of social discrimination, or simply due to ignorance.

Another difficult issue faced by deaf women in the family is related to sexuality and family formation. Although sexuality is considered an essential element of the adult personality, women with disabilities are seen as asexual beings who have no such requirements and who are not sexually desirable to others. This leads to self-image problems, inhibition of sexual desires, and in some cases, the inability to establish relationships. Because of this, is also likely to suffer sexual abuse, as they rarely receive sex education. For a broader reading of this issue, we recommend consulting the chapter on sexuality of people with deafness.

Employment

In relation to employment, inequality of opportunity is reflected in the refusal of the organizations to hire a disabled woman because they think they have little potential, they need help, they will have a lower yield or to consider them incapable of doing the work; after all companies often want to avoid difficulties, for example, possible absence from work caused by disability or having to adapt the workplace to the needs of the deaf (Mun Man Shum,

Conde, and Portillo, 2006). Thus, an aspect that could bring independence, personal fulfillment and social recognition, such as employment becomes another barrier for deaf women to deal with.

Mun Man Shum, Conde and Portillo (2006) reported that 13.2% of people with disabilities have expressed experiences of discrimination in the search, selection and recruitment. Even when they get a job, 30% reported having experienced discrimination of various kinds in the workplace, for example, the company did not fit the job to their needs, discriminatory treatment by their employer or colleagues and receive less salary that a person without a disability. Harassment in the workplace can take various forms, and inequality of opportunity makes the victim feel depressed and afraid of losing their job. Specifically in the case of deaf women, the barriers that affect them the most are the access to information and the ability to inform and be informed, and this makes it difficult to access good jobs and not competing for positions in better conditions.

Education

The lack of equal employment opportunities has its preamble in educational inequality between hearing children and deaf children, since a low level of education and training hinders access to employment and competition for better jobs. The major difficulty for deaf girls is the communication barrier. Deaf people need the mediation of a sign language interpreter to communicate with a hearing person, and deaf children are no exception. A large majority of deaf children and adolescents drop out because they can not follow the normal course of the classes because there are no interpreters in the classroom.

Although school integration programs are intended for inclusion in the school system for pupils with special educational needs, this is a way to ensure that students with disabilities are integrated into regular schools eventually, but true integration with positive results is not always the case. Currently, school integration is the right of all persons with disabilities, but we must take into account that not all mainstream schools are able to manage the support required for the proper development of people with disabilities (Mun Man Shum, Conde, and Portillo, 2006).

In addition to the communication barrier, another difficulty is that parents do not consider that the formation of their daughters with disabilities is important for their future, and are thought to have no potential as women with disabilities.

Use of Public Services

Regarding the field of public services, women with disabilities mentioned some difficulties. First is the paucity of information and lack of adaptation to access information networks, for example, no sign language interpreters in public areas. Second are the barriers of social and attitudinal, that is, public officials, through ignorance or prejudice, are not sensitive to the needs of women with disabilities, and disability status is used as an argument to deny any service. These situations result in that women with disabilities are unable to defend their rights and develop as citizens. Some authors (Estrada, The Violation of Human Rights of Deaf people in Mexico, 2008a) have addressed the problem of the violation of human rights of deaf people in Mexico, concluding that the right to education and health (including mental health) are the most vulnerable rights in our country.

Violence and Abuse in Deaf Women

Torices (2003) notes that women with disabilities are more susceptible to be abused than people without disabilities, in a ratio of two to five. In addition to this ratio, they have higher risk with severe disabilities, and with learning and communication difficulties.

Since this population is likely to be violated, we would expect to find reports of abuse or discrimination, however, is not so. The reasons why deaf women do not report being battered or violated are related to the above paragraphs. First, the majority of deaf women are not aware of abuse, they do not know that violence is something that infringes on their rights and can be reported, nor are aware of existing services that could help them.

Similarly, it is difficult to make a complaint against the agressor because of communication barriers. In government areas, interpreter services in order to communicate their situation are rarely available. In these cases, the option for the deaf woman is to bring a relative or acquaintance to make up for the role of interpreter. However, there is the reluctance of the deaf woman to talk about abuse with someone in their immediate social group, whether deaf or listener. Because the social circle of the deaf woman usually comes down to their partner and associations of the deaf, it is easy for information to be shared and deaf woman may fear stigmatization or discrimination in their own community. Even when they want to complain, the woman with disabilities is often given less credibility.

Communication barriers also complicate report abuse including members of the family. Thus, the deaf woman suffers from a lack of family support, whether their parents are hearing or deaf. In case family members of deaf women are listeners, the communication barrier exists because the deaf person uses sign language and hearing people use spoken language. If the parents or family are deaf, communication barriers are still present but out of the family, causing lack of resources and information necessary to act in an abusive situation. Another reason why it is difficult to report abuse of deaf woman is because she usually is economically dependent on their partner or family. If the deaf woman depends on her partner, he can perceive he is in a lower risk of being discovered and he can continue the abuse or may threaten the victim to withdraw economic support if she decides to report abuse. This situation worsens as discussed in the section on Employment, as deaf women suffer higher unemployment, lower pay wages, and therefore less likely to become independent. In case a deaf woman has managed to report abuse, there are few support services available to meet their needs. For example, the shelters do not have sign language interpreters, specialists for women ignore the needs of abused women with disabilities and both individual and group therapies are designed for hearing women.

As can be seen clearly, the biggest difficulty remains in the communication barrier. Although bilingual education (Spanish and sign language) and having MSL interpreters in public places are constitutional rights of the deaf population (Estrada, 2008a), it is generally not recognized by society or defended by deaf women because they are unaware of them. Therefore, it is essential the publication of information in MSL for deaf women to be aware of their situation, to defend their rights and fight for equal opportunities.

5. Percentages and Statistics of Violence in Deaf Women

In preparing this section we rely on data from the National Survey on Violence Against Women (National Public Health Institute, 2003), the

National Survey on the Dynamics of Household Relationships (ENDIREH,by its spanish acronym) (National Statistics Institute and Geography, 2004a, 2007) and Persons with Disabilities in Mexico: a Census Vision (National Institute of Statistics and Geography, 2004b).

We mentioned earlier that because of various reasons, deaf women are more likely to be violated. However, studies to estimate the violence among women in Mexico until now has not taken into account in this population.

The National Survey on Violence against Women, held in 2003 by the National Institute of Public Health (INSP, by its spanish acronym), was a national survey on violence in women seeking medical care in public institutions (ISSTE, IMSS and SSA) in Mexico. The study subjects were women(15 years old and older), users of public health services and the methodology included the 32 states of the Republic. 26.240 interviews were obtained from health services users. There is no data on whether interviewed women were deaf or had any other disability.

The ENDIREH was made by the National Institute of Statistics and Geography (INEGI), the National Women's Institute (INMUJERES) and the United Nations Fund for Development of Women (UNIFEM) in 2003, with a new uprising in 2006. The theme of 2003 was violence against married women exercised by the husband or partner, while in 2006 other types of violence rose in areas of employment, education, social and heritage, including violence by persons other than the spouse.

In 2006, ENDIREH methodology was proposed that the target population were women aged 15 years or older, randomly selected using the National Housing Framework 2002 obtained from the XII General Census of Population and Housing 2000. Here it is mentioned that the survey results can be generalized to the entire study population, but we did not find evidence that the questionnaire was made to women who are deaf or other disability.

The XII General Census of Population and Housing Census 2000 revealed that nationwide there were 795 million people with disabilities, representing 1.8% of the total population. The most common disability was physical disability, with 45.3%, second is the visual type with 26%, 16.1% were mental type, 15.7% have a hearing impairment and language disability 4.9% (note: the sum of the types of disability may be more than one hundred because of the population with more than one disability). Specifically , it is reported that there are nearly three people per thousand inhabitants in the country in the population with hearing impairment, which means about 281,000 people, with 43.9% being women.

On the other hand, the National Disability Survey, prepared by the Secretariat of Health and the NIPH in 2000 concluded that 2.3% of total Mexican population has a disability, that's about 2.2 million Mexicans, a larger amount than that mentioned in the 2000 Census conducted by the INEGI. The percentage distribution was found: motor impairment, 46.6% mental, 16.5%; hearing, 16.4%, visual, 14.6%, and language, 2.2% (Ministry of Health - National Institute of Public Health, 2000).

Antunez and Balcazar (2005) mention that the XII General Census of Population and Housing 2000 is considered unreliable by the organizations of and for persons with disabilities, and reporting that data are is inferior to reality.

Whether we take into account the population with hearing impairment reported in Census 2000 (approximately 281.800 women and men), or the National Disability Survey 2000 (approximately 360.800 women and men), we wonder how come there are so many deaf people continue to be overlooked in attempts to obtain prevalence, frequency and extent of violence perpetrated against women. Women with disabilities are receiving more abuse than people without disabilities, in a ratio of two to five (Torices, 2003). Torices's article on violence against women with disabilities, is part of the meager material found in Mexico related to violence against deaf women.

Briefly mentioned studies in other countries have a reference to violence against women occurs in greater proportion in the population with disabilities.

The Network of Women with Disabilities in Canada (Ridington, 1989) interviewed 245 women with disabilities and found that 40% had suffered abuse. The attackers were primarily spouses and ex-spouses (37%), strangers (28%), parents (15%), some service providers (10%) and dates (7%). Davis (2000) mentions that the risk of abuse for people with disabilities is 2-5 times higher than people without disabilities. Nosek, Howland, Rintala, Young and Chanpong (2001) report that 62% of women with disabilities have been abused by their intimate partners. Hassouneh-Phillips and Curry (2002) state that an estimated 85% of women with disabilities have been victimized in a relationship at some point in their lives.

As can be seen, the authors differ in the percentage of women with disabilities who have suffered abuse and mistreatment in the proportion of women without disabilities. This difference may be due to different definitions of what constitutes abuse, as well as women with disabilities are a very heterogeneous group and the rates depend on the type of abuse, disability, causes of disability, degree of disability among other variables. However, what is real is that the population of women with hearing impairment are at greater risk of abuse and mistreatment, as evidenced by research and aspects mentioned above in sub Differences between Women's Violence in deaf and hearing.

Based on what was mentioned by Davis (2000) and Torices (2003) on women with disabilities are receiving or are at risk of abuse of 2-5 times more than women without disabilities, can be estimated by violence and abuse in this population based on statistics provided by the National Survey on Violence Against Women (National Public Health Institute, 2003) and ENDIREH 2006 (National Institute of Statistics and Geography, 2007). We should do this because, as mentioned above, currently in Mexico there are surveys that have measured directly on violence and abuse in women who are deaf.

In the National Survey on Violence against Women, when asked "Have you ever experienced in your life a violent relationship?", 25.8% of respondents said yes. The main aggressor was the partner, 74% of cases. When asked "In the last twelve months, the relationship with your boyfriend, husband, partner or last partner is or has been violent?" 8.7% of women answered affirmatively. However, after application of a scale of violence prevalence was 21.5%, more than twice reported before the implementation of the questionnaire. We believe this percentage difference is important because it directly to the question about whether a woman is violated or receiving abuse from her partner can cause a denial of women when the situation has not accepted or is not aware of it. The difference with the scale of violence is specifically questioning whether their partner had beaten, pushed, benchmarking, violent or sexual intercourse against her will, among other things.

Similarly, it is asked when during the woman's life violence had happened or if it was happening at that time. The current partner violence, including any kind of violence perpetuated by the boyfriend, husband or partner in the last twelve months, was reported by 21.5% of women. The violence of life partner, referring to any point in a relationship, although it had already completed more than twelve months, had a prevalence of 34.5%. And the violence ever in life, perpetuated by the couple, family or others from childhood, had prevalence of 60.4%. According to the results, 1 in 5 women suffer violence from their current partner, one of every three couples have experienced violence at some time in their lives and two of every three women have experienced violence at some time in their lives.

Turning now to data obtained by the ENDIREH 2006, reported that 67 of every 100 females age 15 and over have experienced an incident of violence at some level, whetherthe couple, community, work, family or school. The most reported violence was the couple (exercised by the current or last husband or partner) with 43.2%, communal violence was suffered by 39.7% of women, violence at work by 29.9%, 15.9% of family and school 15.6%.

With regard to workplace violence, for every 100 worker women, 24 reported having suffered wage inequities on men for the same level, requests for pregnancy tests, fewer opportunities for promotions, layoffs or reduced wages for pregnancy, by age or marital status, while 12 out of 100 reported having experienced sexual harassment. With regard to intimate partner violence, it is reported that out of 100 women surveyed who have or had a relationship, 38 had suffered emotional violence, economic violence 23, 19 physical and 9 sexual violence.

According to INEGI (2007), the number of intentional deaths of women registered in Mexico in 2006 was 2,011; 1,290 of which were homicides and 713 suicides. This means that six women die every day because of violence: four for homicide and two suicides.

These figures, alarming in itself, would be multiplied by 2-5 fold in women with a disability because of the increased risk of abuse and violence, however, is an invisible reality in these statistics.

6. Consequences of Violence on Women

When talking about the consequences of violence and abuse in the deaf woman, we mean not only the physical injuries inflicted by the aggressor, as there is research that shows that being subjected to a violent relationship has serious health consequences for women both the short and long term. Even physical symptoms that are chronic may be due to nonspecific ill-treatment or be intermingled with them (White, Ruiz-Jarabo, García, and Martín-García, 2004).

Among the reported consequences of violence and abuse are (National Public Health Institute, 2003; Torices, 2003; Mun Man Shum, Conde, and Portillo, 2006):

- Physical trauma. The most common injuries are bruises, abrasions, fractures and broken eardrum.
- Sexual and reproductive health. Sexually transmitted infections, vaginal bleeding, urinary infections, unwanted pregnancies, abortions,

pregnancy complications, pelvic inflammatory disease, difficulty in sexual intimacy.

- Economics. Economic impact due to the use of health services, and labor difficulties. 6.9% of women interviewed by the INSP (2003) reports that had to change jobs and 5.4% have lost their job because of the violence.
- Deterioration of physical health. Partner violence is the third factor, after diabetes and problems of delivery, the more lost years of healthy life is in women. Similarly can be: fibromyalgia, asthma, abdominal pain, sleep difficulties and psychosomatic problems.
- Psychological. Among the consequences commonly detected in the long term are: depression, PTSD, anxiety and battered woman syndrome. These difficulties affect personal self-worth because women internalize prejudice, stereotypes and discrimination, they feel inferior, low self-esteem and low expectations for the future.
- Social and relational. Because of the imposition and manipulation of the husband or partner during the ill-treatment, women had to interrupt their interpersonal relationships and family and sink in a growing isolation. The strategies to confront social discrimination also vary from one woman to another, in some cases lead to difficulties in social interaction and not wanting to leave home because they feel they are not people for whom you can feel affection, interest or attraction; sexual or loving.
- Danger of death. The risk of death in battered women may include intentional or accidental killing by the couple as well as thoughts or attempted suicide because of depression or PTSD.
- Damage to other family members. The consequences of violence are not limited to damages that threaten the physical and psychological integrity of women, but also other family members, especially children, living in an abusive environment and that have high probability internalizing behaviors that perpetuate the living model.

7. First Steps to Stop the Violence

Among the possible responses of women to violence include: face it, denounce it or leave the abuser, however, the situation for battered women is difficult in any of the options. The situation is even more contentious because, for a battered woman deciding between one of these three options and end the abuse, must first be aware of it and decide to end the cycle of violence. As mentioned Mun Man Shum, Conde and Portillo (2006) for women, it is emotionally very difficult to assume that persons in their own family are able to become perpetrators and abusers. According to the Institute of Women (2001), only about one third of battered women have suffered abuse awareness and reported it. This is because some violent behavior remain socially accepted as normal or thought that ill-treatment is a private matter of the family.

In the population of women with disabilities, these are more difficult situations than other women because they are less aware of the abuse, there are few support services available to help them and violence against this group is punished less than in the rest of the population (Wolbring, 1994). Therefore, we consider very important the process of making aware of the abusive situation, because if it does not, the abused woman can not make the decision to confront a situation that threatens her health; both physical and psychological, short and long term. Similarly, it is essential that health personnel are able to identify victims of domestic violence, because commonly nurses or doctors are the first to have contact when women use health services.

Although health professionals, education and directors of hospitals and educational institutions are obliged to report the existence of a domestic violence situation, there are reasons why professionals choose not to highlight it. One is to consider abuse as a private family matter or, believing that the victim would also ask for help if needed or assuming that abuse can not be that bad or otherwise the woman would have left the aggressor (Shipway, 2004). Nosek (quoted in Shipway, 2004) mentions that the reasons for not asking for help are very similar between women with and without disabilities, but in addition, women with disabilities fear the consequences of public disclosure of abuse, especially in the case she is dependent on their partner or perpetrator because of her disability.

In the National Survey on Violence Against Women (National Public Health Institute, 2003) women were asked about what health care team member should be the one to ask about an abusive situation. The 35.2% of women believe that the psychologist, followed by doctors (21.5%) and social worker (20%). 1.7% of women felt that no health professional should ask about abuse, the cause of this was considering it a private matter (66.1%), it is not competent of health personnel (9.7%) or nothing can be done to change the situation (12.9%).

To conclude this section we describe the advice of the Royal College of General Practitioner in the UK, about cases of partner violence. Mainly that no patient should be forced to make a decision. Only a person can decide what is right for her, taking into account their particular situation. It should encourage individual autonomy, self-esteem and self-determination, but their opinion should be respected.

- If the woman is unwilling to return with the aggressor, she should be advised about the services available in local agencies and offer help to contact them.
- If the woman decides to return to the abuser:
  a) Provide address or telephone number of local shelters for women.
  b) Recommend her to save money as well as major financial and legal documents in a safe place in case of emergency.
  c) To help her plan an escape plan in case of emergency.
- If you suspect the possibility that sons and daughters are at risk, seriously consider referral to social services, if possible, with the consent of the patient.

8. Treatment Programs and Psychotherapeutic Techniques

In 2007, the Interior Ministry issued the General Law of Access to Women to a Life Free of Violence, whose main objective was to establish coordination between the Federation, states and municipalities to prevent, punish and eradicate violence against women. He mentioned that the State must take into consideration: (a) provide care, legal advice and free specialized psychological treatment for victims, (2) to provide re-educational services specialized and free for the aggressor to eradicate violent behavior, (3) to avoid that the victim and the offender receive the attention provided by the same person and at the same location, (4) avoid mediation or conciliation procedures, (5) promote the separation and removal of the aggressor respect to the victim and (6) encourage the installation and maintenance of shelters for victims and their children.

Despite the great importance that this law is for victims of domestic violence, as well as for women who suffer or have suffered discrimination in other areas, this law is not commonly known among the general population, much less among the population of deaf women. We believe that the dissemination of this law has not been as extensive as it should be in populations with a greater risk of abuse, referring to women with disabilities. Coupled with the lack of disclosure, are the difficulties of adapting the intervention and treatment programs available to the needs and capacities of women with disabilities.

Additionally, we would like to mention that around August 2009, we visited various organizations in the city of Monterrey and the metropolitan area of Nuevo Leon, in charge of providing support services, legal and psychological treatment for battered women. However, none of them were prepared to help deaf women. Among the difficulties we observed, there were: the misinformation about deaf culture (see chapter on cultural identity), lack of interpreters or ignorance of why they are needed, and that the psychologists and social workers did not know the MSL. We strongly recommend that health professionals have at least a general knowledge of deaf culture and the need for MSL interpreters in hospitals and clinics, because the programs and services available from domestic violence can not be applied to deaf women without adaptation.

In relation to the psychotherapeutic intervention techniques aimed at female victims of violence, there are some that stand out because of its frequent use in programs for battered women. These include: cognitive restructuring, relaxation training, training in communication skills and solving problems, stress inoculation and exposure therapy. Labrador, Fernández-Velasco and Rincon (2006) also recommend treating symptoms associated with PTSD, such as depression, low self-esteem, feelings of guilt and issues of personal and social adjustment.

Similarly, there are measuring instruments commonly used in domestic violence interventions and these can be applied in the pre-treatment, during treatment, the completion of it or follow-up phases. Echeburúa and Corral (2006) suggest to include: :

- Symptom Severity Scale Post-Traumatic Stress Disorder (Echeburúa E., Corral, Amor, Zubizarreta, and Sarasua, 1997).
- State/trait Anxiety Inventory (STAI) (Spielberger, Gorsuch, and Lushene, 1970).
- Beck Depression Inventory (BDI) (Beck, Steer, and Brown, 1996). In the case of this scale in Mexico, Estrada (2008b, 2009) has made cultural adaptations and Spanish Sign Language and MSL of this instrument.

- Self Esteem Scale (Rosenberg, 1965)
- Survey of Treatment Satisfaction (Larsen, Attkinson, Hargreaves, and Nguyen, 1979).
- Perceived Stress Scale (Cohen, Kamarck, and Mermelstein, 1983). In the case of Mexico, is being adapted for Mexican deaf people (see chapter on perceived stress).

Although the application of measuring instruments is something that is widely recommended for the objective evaluation of changes over treatment, unfortunately there are few scales and questionnaires standardized for the deaf. With the exception of the Beck Depression Inventory (Beck, Steer, and Brown, 1996) and the Perceived Stress Scale (Cohen, Kamarck, and Mermelstein, 1983), both adapted by Estrada (2009) to the Mexican deaf, we have knowledged that any other of the scales recommended by Echeburúa and Corral have been adapted to the MSL. The gravity of this situation is realized when deaf, battered women do not seek counseling services because they could not even begin to assess due to the lack of tools tailored to their population.

We would like to mention in this section an article published in Labrador, Fernández-Velasco and Rincon (2006) on the effectiveness of a brief intervention program for female victims of domestic violence. Although his research sample is small (20 participants) we can highlight its brevity, the results and explanation of its content. The treatment program consisted of 8 sessions of 60 minutes, individual format and weekly basis. The basic components of the experimental group were psycho-education, control of diaphragmatic breathing, cognitive therapy and exposure therapy. The authors mention that in pre-treatment evaluation, the entire sample had a diagnosis of chronic post-traumatic stress disorder. In the second assessment, while 100% of the control group continued to present chronic PTSD, 100% of women who completed the program did not meet the minimum cutoff for a diagnosis. Also observed was concomitant clinical improvement in symptoms, although the program was addressed directly only to PTSD.

In relation to the diagnosis of depression, it was present in 90% of the control group, compared with 50% of the experimental group, 100% of the control group presented low scores in self esteem, while in the treatment group, the level drops to 60%, and finally, in the category of maladjustment, it was present in 100% of the control group while it is reduced to 60% in the experimental group. The pros we see in the intervention program, Labrador, Fernández-Velasco and Rincon is first, of its brevity; since the above results were obtained in only two months of weekly sessions. The brevity of treatment helps to overcome the problem as soon as possible and women readjust to society. Secondly, we want to mention the significant reduction of concomitant symptoms without specific treatment existing for it. This highlights the importance of overcoming PTSD in battered women, because when this happens, positively affects other variables. And finally there are the therapeutic techniques that were used, which we believe have the possibility to adapt to MSL.

CONCLUSIONS

The purpose of this chapter was to investigate an issue in today's society; continually listening and its impact on violence against women. However, there were difficulties because our population of interest, deaf women, seems to go unnoticed or be invisible on this issue. When it comes to programs for deaf people, unfortunately, most of them focus only on repairing hearing loss and integrate them into society, taking for granted that the only difficulty they have is the disability and once repaired all their difficulties will be resolved. On the other hand, surveys to assess violence against women in Mexico rarely take into account people with disabilities. In our search, we found a significant number of both government and civilian programs to prevent and treat domestic violence, but found none suitable to the deaf. Therefore, the greatest difficulty we met was the lack of programs, research and data on violence against deaf women.

We consider it essential that mental health professionals know about the deaf culture and to promote interest in research in this population, since it is a subject that is little known and even goes unnoticed in special education. Between the lines of research that could develop health professionals are:

- Programs to raise awareness of the role of the psychologist in the deaf community and offer services tailored to them, for example, having MSL interpreters in therapy.
- Prevention programs offered at LSM, serving the deaf community to report domestic violence and the empowerment of women.
- Standardize scales and questionnaires to deaf people.
- To investigate the psychological treatments that work best for deaf battered women and deaf men offenders.

- Provide training to staff in hospitals and clinics, as well as agents who perform procedures for complaints about the deaf community, and the importance of having interpreters of MSL in these places, as is commonly thought that all deaf read lips, use oral or read written Spanish.

The relation between mental health and deafness is an issue that begins to develop in Mexico, and because of this, there is a vast field of research available. However, we think that the health professional always go hand in hand with the deaf community, that because the hearing society has generally taken the deaf person as a disabled person who needs to hear and learn to talk at all costs . We believe that deafness itself is not a problem, but the difficulty occurs when they hit the listener and the deaf culture, and when one of them wants to impose on the other. That is why it is of utmost importance to health professionals working together and in cooperation with the deaf community.

As a line, we can discuss further research awareness to the general public about disability. We were surprised by data that showed the First National Survey on Discrimination in Mexico (Antúnez and Balcazar, 2005), where 41% of respondents considered that people with disabilities do not work as well as others, 37% felt that schools where there are many children with disability, decreased quality of teaching and 42% agreed that given the difficulties in employment that are currently in Mexico, it would be preferable to give work to people without disabilities than those with a disability.

Results such as these, unfortunately, demonstrate a lack of education and understanding that has the average citizen about people with disabilities. Despite the large number of laws and reforms issued on behalf of people with disabilities, lack of education of society can only be overcome with information, whether to inform the general public on the equality of persons with disabilities, as well as letting know people with disabilities about their rights so they can be defended.

Specifically in relation to violence against women who are deaf, our recommendations focus on the need to make them aware of their rights to live a life free of violence through awareness and prevention campaigns through MSL. It is equally important to provide information about available services and programs for victims of abuse, stressing that a violent relationship is not something to be hidden or bear, but a crime.

REFERENCES

Antúnez, M., and Balcázar, A. (2005). *Diagnóstico sobre Discapacidad en México. Consejo Nacional para Prevenir la Discriminación.* Recuperado el 31 de Julio de 2009, de Secretaria de Conferencias y Reuniones: http://scm.oas.org/pdfs/2007/DIL00140s.pdf

Beck, A., Steer, R., and Brown, G. (1996). *Manual for the Beck Depression Inventory-II.* San Antonio: Psychological Corporation.

Blanco, P., Ruiz-Jarabo, C., García, L., and Martín-García, M. (2004). La violencia de pareja y la salud de las mujeres. *Gaceta Sanitaria , 18*, 182-188.

Brodwin, M., and Siu, F. (2007). Domestic Violence Against Women Who Have Disabilites: What Educators Need To Know. *Education , 127* (4), 548-551.

Camara de Diputados. (2005). *Ley General de las Personas con Discapacidad.* Recuperado el 31 de Julio de 2009, de Diario Oficial de la Federación: http://www.cddhcu.gob.mx/LeyesBiblio/pdf/LGPD.pdf

Cohen, S., Kamarck, T., and Mermelstein, R. (1983). A global measure of perceived stress. *Journal of Health and Social Behavior , 24*, 385-396.

Davis, L. (2000). Feature Issue on Violence Against Women with Developmental or Other Disabilities. *Impact , 13* (3), 8-9.

Deschner, J. (1984). *How to end the hitting habit.* New York: Free Press.

Echeburúa, E., and Corral, P. (2006). *Manual de Violencia Familiar* (Cuarta ed.). Madrid: Siglo XXI.

Echeburúa, E., Corral, P., Amor, P., Zubizarreta, I., and Sarasua, B. (1997). Escala de Gravedad de Síntomas del Trastorno de Estrés Postraumático: Propiedades Psicométricas. *Análisis y Modificación de Conducta , 23*, 503-526.

Echeburúa, E., Corral, P., Sarasua, B., and Zubizarreta, I. (1996). Tratamiento Cognitivo-Conductual del Trastorno por Estrés Postraumático Crónico en Víctimas de Maltrato Doméstico: Un Estudio Piloto. *Análisis y Modificación de Conducta , 22* (85), 627-654.

Estrada, B. (2008a). La vulneración de los derechos humanos de las personas Sordas en México. *Revista del Centro Nacional de Derechos Humanos , 3* (8), 105-127.

Estrada, B. (2008b). *Salud Mental, Depresión y Sordera.* Monterrey: Universidad Autónoma de Nuevo León.

Estrada, B. (2009). Metodología para la Adaptación de Instrumentos de Evaluación Psicológica a la Lengua de Señas Mexicana. En J. Moral,

Investigaciones en Psicología Social, Personalidad y Salud. Monterrey: Universidad Autónoma de Nuevo León.

García-Moreno, C. (2000). *Violencia contra la mujer. Género y equidad en la salud.* Washington: Organización Panamericana de la Salud y Harvard Center for Population and Development Studies.

Gondolf, E., and Fisher, E. (1988). *Battered women as survivors : an alternative to treating learned helplessness.* Lexington: Lexington Books.

Hassouneh-Phillips, D., and Curry, M. (2002). Abuse of women with disabilites: State of the science. *Rehabilitation Counseling Bulletin , 45,* 96-104.

Heise, L., Ellsberg, M., and Gottemoeller, M. (1999). Para acabar con la violencia contra la mujer. *Population Reports , 4* (11).

Iniesta, A. (2004). *La Mujer Sorda en la Vida Privada y Pública.* Alicante: Centro de Estudios sobre la Mujer.

Instituto de la Mujer. (2001). *Las mujeres en cifras del 1996-2000.* Madrid: Instituto de la Mujer.

Instituto Nacional de Estadística y Geografía. (2004a). *Encuesta Nacional sobre la Dinámica de las Relaciones en los Hogares 2003, ENDIREH.* México: INEGI.

Instituto Nacional de Estadística y Geografía. (2007). *Encuesta Nacional sobre la Dinámica de las Relaciones en los Hogares 2006, ENDIREH.* México: INEGI.

Instituto Nacional de Estadística y Geografía. (2004b). *Las personas con discapacidad en México: una visión censal.* México: INEGI.

Instituto Nacional de Salud Pública. (2003). *Encuesta Nacional sobre Violencia contra las Mujeres.* México: INSP.

Kelly, L. (2000). ¿Cómo en casa en ninguna parte? La violencia doméstica, la seguridad de las mujeres y los niños y la responsabilidad de los hombres. *Carpeta de Documentos del Foro Mundial de Mujeres contra la Violencia* (págs. 25-36). Valencia: Centro Reina Sofía para el Estudio de la Violencia.

Labrador, F., Fernández-Velasco, M., and Rincón, P. (2006). Eficacia de un programa de intervención individual y breve para el trastorno por estrés postraumático en mujeres víctimas de violencia doméstica. *International Journal of Clinical and Health Psychology , 6* (3), 527-547.

Larsen, D., Attkinson, C., Hargreaves, W., and Nguyen, T. (1979). Assessment of Client/Patient Satisfaction: Development of a General Scale. *Evaluation and Program Planning , 2* (3), 197-207.

Mun Man Shum, G., Conde, Á., and Portillo, I. (2006). *Mujer, discapacidad y violencia. El rostro oculto de la desigualdad.* Madrid: Instituto de la Mujer.

Nosek, A., Howland, C., Rintala, D., Young, M., and Chanpong, G. (2001). National study of women with physical disabilites: Final report. *Sexuality and Disability , 19* (1), 5-39.

Pagelow, M. (1997). Battered women: A historical research and some common myths. *Journal of Aggression, Maltreatment and Trauma , 97* (I), 97-116.

Ridington, J. (1989). *Beating the odds: Violence and women with disabilities (Position Paper 2).* Vancouver: DisAbled Women's Network.

Rosenberg, M. (1965). *Society and the Adolescent Self-Image.* Princeton: Princeton University Press.

Secretaría de Gobernación. (2007). *Decreto por el que se expide la Ley General de Acceso de las Mujeres a una Vida Libre de Violencia.* Recuperado el 31 de Julio de 2009, de Diario Oficial de la Federación: http://www.diputados.gob.mx/LeyesBiblio/pdf/LGAMVLV.pdf

Secretaría de Salud - Instituto Nacional de Salud Pública. (2000). *Encuesta Nacional de Salud. Cuestionario de Hogar.* México: SSA-INSP.

Seligman, M. (1975). *Helplessness: On Depression, Development, and Death.* San Francisco: Freeman.

Shainess, N. (1979). Vulnerability to Violence: Masochism as Process. *American Journal of Psychotherapy , 33*, 174-189.

Shipway, L. (2004). *Domestic Violence: A Handbook of Health Professionals.* New York: Routledge.

Spielberger, C., Gorsuch, R., and Lushene, R. (1970). *Manual for the State-Trait Anxiety Inventory.* Palo Alto: Consulting Psychologist Press.

Torices, I. (2003). *Violencia contra las mujeres con discapacidad.* México: Comisión Nacional de Derechos Humanos.

Vázquez, B. (1999). Evaluación psicológica de la mujer maltratada. *Clínica y Salud , 10* (3), 377-391.

Walker, L. (1999). Psychology and Domestic Violence Around the World. *American Psychologist , 54* (1), 21-29.

Walker, L. (1979). *The Battered Woman.* New York: Harper and Row, Publishers, Inc.

Walker, L. (2009). *The Battered Woman Syndrome* (Third ed.). New York: Springer Publishing Company.

Wolbring, G. (1994). *Violence and Abuse in the Lives of People with Disabilities*. Recuperado el 31 de Julio de 2009, de BroadReach; Training and Resources: http://www.normemma.com/artfvioabu.htm

Zubizarreta, I., Sarasua, B., Echeburúa, E., Corral, P., Sauca, D., and Emperanza, I. (1994). Consecuencias psicológicas del maltrato doméstico. En E. Echeburúa, *Personalidades violentas* (págs. 29-152). Madrid: Pirámide.

Chapter 3

SEXUALITY OF PEOPLE WITH DEAFNESS: APPLICATION OF A SEX EDUCATION PROGRAM

Georgina Mitre Fajardo and Benito Estrada Aranda

ABSTRACT

The sexuality of the deaf and other disabled groups is thrown into taboos, false beliefs and fears, caused mainly by lack of knowledge on the subject. The limited literature on these issues limit opportunities to offer such services to the deaf groups from various disciplines. Deaf people are able to interact sexually with others in the same way hearing people do, their ability to manifest sexually is not affected at most levels through which the deaf can experience their sexuality. The reaction of the deaf to the discovery of their sexuality and their reaction to sex does not have specific characteristics as a result of hearing impairment. However, when talking about sexuality, both deaf people as well as listeners, we are talking not only of an independent, but a specific part of the overall structure of the individual, seen as a unit, and sexuality comes from pregnancy and unfolds under the specific structure of each individual. Therefore, the reality of sexual development of deaf people is disturbed by some features that involve these groups, as they are, communication barriers (even within the same family), lack of sexual education or limited social relationships generally established.

In this chapter we describe some models in the literature, that represent the way in which regularly deaf people deal with interpersonal relationships and partner relationships, as well as some factors that makes this group more vulnerable to abuse and unwanted pregnancies. We also describe the process of implementing a sexual education program offered to a group of deaf people, where we could meet real and current needs surrounding this population in the area of sexuality; needs that can and should motivate changes to achieve a better quality of sexual life of deaf people.

INTRODUCTION

The United Nations Organization (UN) is to ensure the sexual rights of persons with disabilities, through some criteria to its member states.

People with disabilities must not be denied the opportunity to experience their sexuality, having sex or having children. Taking into account that persons with disabilities may experience difficulties in getting married and setting up a family, States should promote the establishment of appropriate counseling services. People with disabilities must have the same access as other methods of family planning, as well as accessible information on sexual functioning of their body.

States should promote measures to change negative attitudes towards marriage, sexuality and parenthood of persons with disabilities, especially girls and women with disabilities, which still prevail in society. It should urge the media to play an important role in removing such negative attitudes.

People with disabilities and their families need to be fully informed about precautions to take against sexual abuse and other forms of abuse. People with disabilities need to be educated on how to avoid it so they can recognize when they have been victims and report on such cases. (P.177)

Despite these guidelines presented by the UN, our societies have not kept pace when it comes to the sexuality of people with disabilities. Families speak little about sexuality to a disabled child and society in general, full of taboos, prejudices and false beliefs, limit, block or prevent people with disabilities, opportunities to manifest emotionally and sexually. It is a deeply rooted belief that by hiding the issue of sexuality, it eliminates the "problem", forgetting the nature of curiosity and the sexual instinct, that is natural in all human beings.

The ability of people with disabilities to have sexual relations, is in no way affected, only limited in some physical, sensory and / or mental way at different levels. People with disabilities have the same emotions and sexual impulses as people without disabilities.

The sexuality of people with disabilities has always been a topic which is preferred not to be spoken. This has led to a myriad of false beliefs and fears, which is rarely discussed and little is known. Masters, Johnson, Biggs and Kolodny (1982) in his "Handbook of Human Sexuality" speak of the discrepancies between the ideal of health services and actual program designed for people with disabilities, and state that until very recently, addressing the problems of sexuality in this population has focused primarily on reproduction, ignoring or minimizing the social and emotional aspects; whereas this lack of attention stems from cultural and social attitudes associated with youth sexuality, vigor and physical attractiveness. These authors consider that the limited research also contributes to the lack of involvement by health professionals interested in this phase of patient care, who had little physiological information to give precise rules to follow.

An unfortunate reality is that people with disabilities often lack information about their sexuality and it places them at disadvantage and makes them more vulnerable to risks such as sexual abuse or unwanted pregnancy.

What we see now in Mexico is a general delay in terms of sexual education for people with disabilities in general, unlike other countries where there are emerging positive changes in services offered to people with disabilities, through which may have more and better opportunities to live healthy and with a satisfactory sexuality. For example, in Spain, the National Federation of the Deaf of Spain (CNSE) published in 2003 (coinciding with the European Year of People with Disabilities) a glossary of Spanish Sign Language (SSL) under the topic Health: Sexuality. This glossary is an important tool to enhance knowledge and increase the possibilities of communication between hearing impaired people on sexuality. Communication, knowledge, education, counseling, are some ways to make a big leap towards full integration of the sexual life of persons with disabilities.

The human sexual expression, including people with disabilities, is vital for participation involved in different aspects and processes of development in humans. Some processes and areas in which it participates, according to some authors (Lopez, 1984; Gómez-Zapiain, 1999, Lopez-Ibor, 1981) are:

- In the balanced structuring of the personality.
- A source of self-knowledge, because through it, the person with disability knows the overall performance of their body, their mind. Through desires, feelings of love, affection and tenderness, they know pleasure.

- In the psychological balance of individuals, as people seek to satisfy the basic need for sexuality, integrated in physical and psychological needs and the inability to do so may cause a temporary or chronic psychological imbalance.
- It is also a source of greater happiness.
- It can enhance and realize the emotional and sexual ability.
- Part of development and personal maturity.
- It is a real option for an image of normal life.
- A source of pleasure, health and welfare.

1. Sexuality and Disability

For the World Health Organization (WHO), disability is any restriction or lack (resulting from an impairment) of ability to perform an activity in the manner or within the range considered normal for a human being (UN, 1983).

For Gomez Zapiain (1999), sexuality is an existential reality, therefore, inherent to the person, any person, regardless of their status. However, a review of the literature on the subject of sexuality and disability shows us that even though there are interesting studies that include both concepts, they are only focused on some specific disabled populations. Talking about disability and sexuality is reduced to only three or four populations with specific disabilities among which are mental retardation, spinal cord injury and some types of sensory impairment from a very broad sense.

For Lopez (1984) sexuality is how we integrate and express our desires and behaviors in different levels of sex, but essentially these levels: genetic sex, gonadal sex, genital sex, somatic sex, hypothalamic-pituitary and psycho-social sex.

Taking this definition as a reference, a person with disabilities needs to be unable to manifest in desire or in behavior, all these levels of sex in order to affirm that people with disabilities are asexual "that do not have sex" as often is thought. It is possible that because of their handicap, any of these levels of sex are affected or distorted, but this does not mean that other levels of sex does not exist. Sanchez and De Pinto (2000) mention that genital function is part of sexuality , however, its alteration does not mean the loss of it.

For his part, López-Ibor (1981) explains the nature of sex as a biological reality, psychological and cultural and states that sexual satisfaction is not a "luxury of nature" but a need deeply embedded in the bowels of men and women. The sexuality of people with disabilities, therefore, is in their body, their mind, in context, part of the cultural fabric of the environment around them, a way that sometimes would not provide the necessary assistance to satisfy their sexual needs.

Although today it is moving slowly to improve the situation of persons with disabilities to successfully live their sexuality, there are still many barriers that impede it, and here we mention some of the most important:

1. The factors involved in people with disabilities, including significant cognitive deficits that distort reality (eg difficulty in categorizing sexes: attraction to both sexes), sexual behaviors that are inappropriate at certain times and settings, inappropriate social behavior, attitudes towards sexuality .certain times and settings, inappropriate social behavior, attitudes towards sexuality.
2. Barriers in society: stereotypes, prejudices, taboos and mis conceptions.
3. Institutional barriers: lack of space and time for privacy, a protected environment, outdated models of intervention (eg, models that do not prepare for integration into the community).
4. Barriers by professionals: The belief that people have a sexuality sleeping and it's best not to wake her, lack of information on sexuality, lack of effective guidelines for the handling or intervention appearance for some situations with sexual manifestations that cause fears, and belief that parents do not accept or cooperate in programs of sex education.
5. The attitudes of parents: The overprotection, excessive fears to pregnancy, sexually transmitted diseases, sexual abuse, denial to integration in standard environments, avoiding spaces and private moments, their children away from friends posing a risk of emotional and sexual relationship.
6. Physical barriers in certain contexts that limit access to standard social interaction contexts.

1.1. Disability: Increased Vulnerability to Abuse, Harassment and Rape

We will present very briefly some reasons why it is considered more vulnerable to people with disabilities, to abuse, harassment and rape, citing some reasons proposed by López (2002) in his book "Sex and Affection for people with disabilities:

- Reduced power of autonomy, which makes them more dependent on others: family members, friends, neighbors, educators and other professionals.
- They have less discriminating capacity to realize what the aggressor intends, so they are more easily deceived and manipulated.
- They have less ability to defend, to say NO when it is something they do not like and, above all, to say it effectively.
- They have been taught to rely and trust in adults.
- They are educated and learn that they have to obey adults with authoritarian forms of discipline.
- They have the typical curiosity of people who do not receive information about sexuality.
- Usually they have no training and ignore almost everything about sexuality.
- They might not have the ability to label a sexual abuse as abuse, may take time to do it, not report it, and even come to view as a positive behavior toward them.
- The offender may be perceived as a friend, as someone who wants them, this is because the abuses occur very often in a context of "affection."
- Not enough security to protect themselves from abuse by other students.
- Many people have direct access to their body to help some other things.

2. Sexuality and Deafness

The literature is very scarce, so it is difficult to know for sure what the sexual development of people with hearing loss, limitations, and what advantages and disadvantages are involved. Through literature we can be witnesses of the prejudices that have existed over the centuries about the relationship between the physical and emotional in people. Myklebust says (1964, 1971) in this regard, that during the Greco-Roman empire they deprived the physical, so they had little tolerance for physical deficiencies. They imagined that a crippled body, could only accommodate a disabled mind.

These feelings of mental abnormality associated with physical disabilities are applied equally to those with a sensory impairment, such as deafness. Although today there is more knowledge about hearing impairment and more tolerance of human diversity, there are still barriers to fully integrate deaf people into society and have equal opportunities. It is necessary to bear in mind that when we speak of people with hearing disabilities, we are referring to a heterogeneous group of people, about various hearing characteristics, such as the type of hearing loss etiology, of age or loss, personal characteristics and social characteristics, making it very difficult to establish a profile or specific pattern of development in this population, however, there are faithful approximations made from many studies.

Moreover, as mentioned by Moreno (2000), there is very little literature directly produced by deaf people where they express, how they see themselves and their opinions about what they want society to offer them to meet their specific needs, allowing them participate on equal terms with the same rights and same duties. However, some authors suggest that when deaf people talk about themselves, they have in mind something more than the audiological status.

For Moreno (2000), the deaf person is one who has a hearing loss, to varying degrees, which is part of the deaf community, accompanied by an identification with the other components of the same group, because among other reasons, share common experiences and a system of communication: sign language. This is the most important, along with others, of what these call deaf culture.

Some authors have collected definitions of "deaf community" from direct reports of deaf people, so, Estrada (2003) got in Spain the following definition:

> "Community for deaf people. They help each other, know Spanish sign language and defend it. Group of people who struggle to overcome communication barriers, they collaborate, participate and learn. It is a place where we are appreciated and know how to understand us, it is a form of communication and unity for all deaf. A group of reference and identification, a way of being in contact with deaf people. We have the same problems and difficulties and share the same culture. It is our own identity. "

It is wrong to believe that sexuality of the deaf is different from the listeners. Consider only the fact that they are different situations in which the deaf can be found when facing the issue of sexuality and different environment in which he moves, and finally, unlike the way in which the deaf learn the world of sexuality. That's why Pinedo (1981) has long stated that the change to the sexual, which occurred in Spain in those years, did not know how it would be assimilated by the deaf and the hearing itself can be considered sufficient in many cases to resolve some doubts, but there are details that were outside the extent of understanding of the "deaf and dumb."

Talking about sexuality is a complex and not always easy, both for parents and educators, because it is accessible to issues of privacy and require a special touch. It is difficult to find that in families of listeners, parents talk about sexuality with their children, even more difficult, finding hearing parents with deaf children talking about the subject. According Giglioli (1994), few people talk about sex to their deaf children, the situation becomes more complex, mainly due to communication barriers. At least between 90 and 95% (Marchesi, 1999) of deaf people are born into hearing families, increasing the possibility of domestic communication barriers. When the parents' response to a question from a deaf child is incomplete, or fail, usually the child does not insist on the question and waiver of the same curiosity. It is important to emphasize that the situation improves when one or both parents are deaf, because they can communicate seamlessly through sign language, disappearing barriers of family communication, in this situation the only factor that could affect would be the level of expertise in sexuality that the deaf parent has and can transmit to their child .

In humans, an important part of sexuality is learned from others, their behaviors, their actions and the messages they send us (the parents first) In this sense, it is important to have good models for good learning, and therefore a sexual functioning. Giglioli (1999) suggests that education and sexual information is given to children from an early age, naturally with the models and language appropriate to the conditions and characteristics of the child.

Pinedo (1981) states: "Our educators of the deaf, look here to ignore this item, or pass a back seat to other training issues that arise and to which preference is given" (p. 73). The same author believes that sex should be fully treated as something natural in the same way that everything around him, because the reaction of the deaf community before the discovery of sexuality, does not represent any special features and their behavior towards sex is equal that of hearing people, with no abnormalities or deviations own or as a result of hearing impairment. Masturbation, homosexuality and sexual aberrations are given in percentages nearly identical to those of the listeners. However, the lack of information and explanations, appropriate to their specific needs, create in the deaf person confused and absurd interpretations of sexuality, often made by other deaf peers that are also unaware of or misunderstand many topics related to sexuality. Poor sex education leads to misconceptions and fantasies.. The deaf homosexual on the other hand, is more difficult. with misconceptions caused by deafness and also those caused by homosexuality. The deaf child as a result of ignorance on issues of sexuality, is left to itself, and may fall into abnormal reactions, such as trauma, frigidity, aberrations (Pinedo, 1981). This same author also believes that ignorance in the sexual field, expands on some deaf people the sense of modesty, markedly impaired, especially girls, to promote the idea of sex as humiliating for them and secondly by encouraging aggression and machismo in the child. The rigid separation of children in schools for the deaf, until recent years, also happened to be aggravating for future social relations between the sexes. Giglioli (1994) argues that knowledge of the boy from the world of women, and vice versa, determines a number of curiosities for the deaf, but occurs late. For deaf people this happens between 16 and 18, whereas for deaf women occur between 18 and 20 years old, in some cases, they never do not access. Deaf people are usually very timid towards issues of sexuality, because of their insecurities of assimilation and difficulties of expression, however, there are exceptions. According to Pinedo (1981) the constant search for images, makes pornography and eroticism, arouse curiosity and attraction of the deaf and writes: *"It is not here so much morbidity as natural curiosity, the need to know before the loss almost no sex education always received" (p. 79).* Some authors (Estrada, 2009) have reviewed data on abuse and trauma in children who are deaf, offered by the National Child Traumatic Stress Network (2006), found some factors that may encourage abuse in people with deafness:

1. Deaf children are more vulnerable than hearing children to suffer emotional abuse, physical, psychological and sexual (Sullivan, Vernon, and Scanlan, 1987).
2. 50% of deaf girls have been sexually abused compared with 25% of girl listeners (Sullivan, Vernon, and Scanlan, 1987).
3. 54% of deaf children have been sexually abused, compared with 10% of hearing children (Sullivan, Vernon, and Scanlan, 1987).
4. In the United States, for every 1,000 children, approximately two or three children are born deaf or with hearing loss (National Institute on Deafness and Other Communication Disorders, 2005). 90% of deaf children are born into families with hearing parents (Padden and Humphries, 1988), other authors point to 95% (Marchesi, 1999), which makes difficult communication within the family.

5. Deaf children are going through many difficulties in learning to read, write, and communicate with the hearing world around them. This is precisely one of the factors that make this population more vulnerable to abuse in general.
6. The average reading of deaf adults is at a level of between fourth and sixth grade core (Traxler, 2000).

2.1. Variables Determinants of Deafness that May Define the Development of Sexuality

Just as every culture marks its own guidelines, deafness may have specific consequences as appropriate, specific consequences should not lose sight of when analyzing the effect of deafness on the development of the individual. To Valmaseda (1995), a hearing loss of any kind, interacts unpredictably in all those factors that distinguish people from one other (such as personality, motivation, and socio-economic conditions of family and social environment). When studying the influence of hearing loss in any aspect of the person, both subject variables and the interaction between them must be present, as well as environment variables. In the table below is presented an outline of these variables.

Table 1. Outline of the variables in the deaf

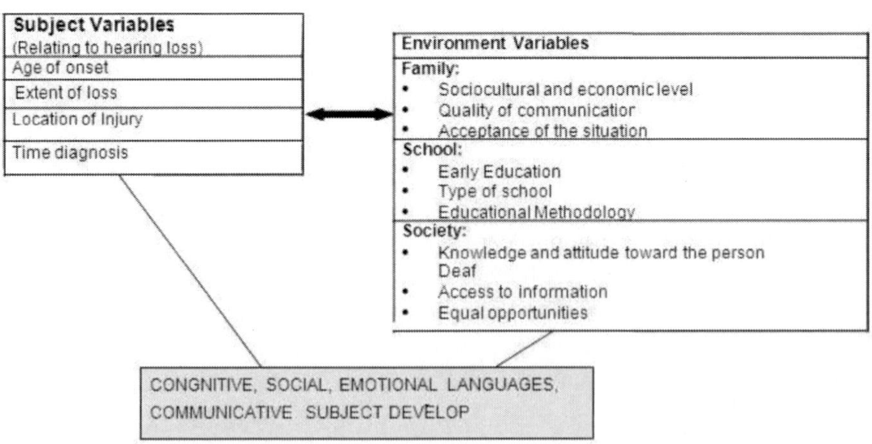

We believe that talking about the sex of any person who is deaf or listener does not mean to speak of an independent, but a specific part of the overall structure of the person seen as a unit. Sexuality so, parts from pregnancy and unfolds under the specific structure of each individual.

Some specific social factors that we believe may affect the sexual development of the deaf person are:

- The social perception of deafness:
    1. Lack of information on the implications of deafness.
    2. A devalued view of the person concerned regarding, for example, their level of intellectual development and their psychic abilities.
- A set of communication barriers at different levels of the social relation of the deaf person to the world of hearing people.
- Existence of misunderstanding, and that deafness unlike other disabilities, is not visible, so the listener may have interpreted his silence as contempt or lack of attention, and react accordingly.
- The oral language of the deaf. For the uninformed hearing person, oral issue of the individual is so abnormal that often leads him to conclude that the communication is not possible and interrupts it.
- The deaf person usually does not have access to information from books, magazines, movies, television, is unable to resort to such facilities, and is limited in order to discover and learn about sexuality itself.
- Medical assistance as regards to the sexual field is very limited, because due to lack of sign language in most of the doctors, they can only deal with them in writing. You can jump in a deaf interpreter who explains the statement made by the doctor but the explanation is often not understood. The deaf person then uses , not their parents or relatives, but others familiar with the deaf sign language and oral language, so sacrificing their privacy to each other.
- The deaf person is very sensitive to what is said, tends to trust people, guessing by the fact that the person trying to communicate with him is making a great effort that values and seeks to respond to his way. This can be a double-edged sword, if that person does not make good use of his influence or trust in the deaf person..
- One immediate problem the deaf has to face when trying to go in search of a mate, is the limitation of choice and meeting places.
- The independence of young deaf people is limited by parents sometimes apprehensive and fearful of the fact that the child needs and can not communicate with them.

- Some hearing parents are unhappy with their deaf children attending to other deaf children and make them be alone with listeners by force, excited in this way to have a more normal life for their child.

2.2. Qualities of the Deaf as a Couple

According to Giglioli (1994), some particular qualities of the deaf as a couple are:

1. All deaf people are generally more willing to face sacrifices because they are accustomed to daily difficulties.
2. Deaf girls have a greater sense of family and the same responsibilities.
3. The vast majority of deaf people are watching what happens around them and have great desire to learn.
4. Deaf people are less prejudiced, and alter the truth of things.
5. The deaf are less influential to the hype and distortions to the media.
6. In the deaf, sexual acts are more instinctive and have fewer problems.

The deaf are less subject to some sexual pathologies characteristic of modern society, such as impotence due to stress, dysfunction caused by prejudice, among others. Not surprisingly, the difficulties of certain explanations along with some limitations imposed by body language, help to create among deaf people an image of sex as something exceedingly physiological. According to Pinedo (1981), some marriages of the deaf are pairedonly to satisfy their sexual desires, or granted fundamental importance to this aspect. Also, you may receive another possibility: a marriage fast, hurried, with restricted options for choosing a partner (someone of the same association) and without first studying the situation of marriage, which often causes malfunctions on marriage. Any deaf person can address the world of listeners in search of partners and in that case the chances of meeting are many, which means are the same as listeners.

Although, as said by Giglioli (1994), the encounter and the frequency of meetings at the hearing person involves a whole series of problems and conditions that the young deaf boy or deaf girl do not want, and sometimes can not afford, limiting their social circle for people who are in their own conditions, and so commonly choose a candidate among those who regularly attend the circle..

Table 1. Questions made by Deaf people

AIDS	If I am HIV positive, can I continue to have sex? Is it safe to kiss a person with HIV who has a wound in the mouth? Can you get AIDS by the bite of a mosquito? What is HIV?
Sexual Desire	After pregnancy, I have increased sexual desire.Iis it normal? I am old and I have no sexual desire. Is this more of a problem?
Masturbation	Is it wrong to masturbate? I've been told that masturbation consumes the spinal cord and intelligence, is it true? Is masturbation a bad option before a sports competition?
Sexual relationship	When is the best time for a boy or a girl to have sex?
Frigidity	I have become frigid after the birth of my son, is it a normal thing? My husband says I'm frigid but it is not true, and he is always in a hurry. What do you have to about that ?
Menstruation	He does not like when I have menstrual blood, but now I like, what I can do? (The woman wants to have sex during menstruation)
Premature Ejaculation	I always come too soon, is that something I have to do?
Prostitution	Is it dangerous to go to prostitutes?
Contraceptive methods	What problems are there t from the pill?
Menopause	There are three months that I am not in menopause, can I have free sex?
Homosexuality	I have had sex in college, can I become homosexual?
How do we act with our children towards sexuality?	What else should I do if my child enters the room while I am making love?

Another option for the deaf is to travel to see different circles, but many of them are restricted in their ability to travel alone for various reasons. This limited choice between the deaf completely changes the way they relate with their partner , and therefore the mode of action in the field of sexuality. On the other hand, the deaf girl recorded, according to Pinedo (1981), a fairly high percentage of coldness compared with the listeners, therefore according to the author of this lack of sexual education and mutual ignorance between the sexes. Moreover,the same author tells us that prostitution among deaf women is v in very small proportions, like lesbianism. Giglioli (1994) believes that the deaf have any advantage in the field of sexuality, believes there are positive things that come from being more or less isolated from the sounds andwords of the outside world.

The author tells us about "words and rumors that sometimes create problems for the listener", which determine the problems that some dysfunctions, or diseases that afflict the listeners rarely occur in the world of the deaf. To Pinedo (1981), sexual awareness of the deaf has a totally materialistic determinants and explains the matter: "The young adult does not usually see in sex, unfortunately, but an animal act for their own pleasure. The young deaf with an astonishing lack of knowledge and ignorance, without exception, beautifully reacts to her motherhood, but by instinct, and that leads to it with almost no preparation. " (P. 81)

On the other hand, in couples who are deaf-listener is very suspicious, according to Giglioli (1994), talking to deaf people in general, is a substantial mistrust of such relationship, although undoubtedly there are couples of this kind that work well and they are happy. According to Giglioli, here we are in the field of relationships that need study, because in such situations have found a number of biases which call for a profound reflection.

Questioning of Deaf People on Issues of Sexuality

(Text requires English translation)

3. Application of a Sex Education Program for Deaf People

The main objective of our study was to implement a sex education program for people with hearing impairment, assessing the level of information about sexuality from the people who made up the sample prior to and subsequent to our intervention (Sexual Education Program).

We previously conducted a studydetecting the needs and demands of existing sex education for people with hearing impairment that could thus be informed of the real needs, we design the content of a sex education program.

The sample of people with hearing impairment of this study was obtained from a public assistance to persons with disabilities in Spain, who allowed us to do this study with a group of deaf people.

A total of 12 hearing impaired people, who are currently conducting training courses at the center, constituted the sample. Of the 12 people who make our sample, seven of them are women and five of them are men. All team members are aged between 19 and 27 years. Everyone in the group are unmarried and without children.

As for the people, audiological data of this study are described as follows:

- 11 people in the group have a prelocutive profoundly deaf and 1 is hard of hearing.
- The ages at which deafness was acquired ranges from 0 to 2 years of age.
- One person said that the cause of his deafness is hereditary; five people claim that they acquired deafness from birth, so it can be prenatal or neonatal origin, five people claim that the cause of their deafness was an infection and one person does not know the cause of his deafness.

The communication aspects of people in this study are described as follows:

- Eight members of the group learned Spanish sign language within an age range between 3 and 17 years.
- To communicate at home, five people in the group use sign language to communicate combining oral (lip reading) and seven members of the group used oral language only (lip reading). One person from each group-mode previously used natural gestures as supplement.
- To communicate with hearing people, eight people in the group used oral language only (lip reading) and three of the group combines oral (lip reading) and sign language. One of these three people also use natural gestures to complement their communication. One person in the group used only natural gestures to communicate with listeners.

To carry out this study, some instruments were applied to deaf people who participated in it, described below:

a) Screening Questionnaire rfor the Need of Sexual Education for Deaf People

The questionnaire was developed with the aim of knowing the personal characteristics of the members of the sample and to detect some sexual education needs. This questionnaire is divided into two sections and consists of 30 questions, mostly multiple choice closed questions and other open questions.

The first section contains personal data, audiological features, communication features and studies, among other things. This first section consists of 22 mostly closed questions with multiple choice or several answers to each case and some open questions.

The second section consists of eight closed questions mostly multiple choice and some open questions. This questionnaire is based on the questionnaire proposed by Baen (1973), who raised seven open questions, we adapted in this study to facilitate the reader's understanding and make more practical answers.

This section aims to determine some characteristics of sex education people have received and detect sexual education needs of people in our sample.

Following the completion of the questionnaire, it was reviewed by a team of interpreters from the center of attention of people with disabilities, who advised us to correct and improve the adaptation of the questionnaire to better understand the group of people with impaired hearing.

b) Questionnaire Assessment of Knowledge About Sexuality

The aim of this questionnaire is to assess and compare the background and knowledge after our intervention (sex education program.)

(Text needs English translation) Este cuestionario contiene los temas que se trataron durante el programa de educación sexual.

Está formado por ocho preguntas cerradas de opción múltiple y se hizo expresamente para este programa de educación sexual. Este cuestionario se aplicó antes y después de nuestra intervención, es decir, antes y después de llevar a cabo el programa de educación sexual, de esta forma pudimos evaluar los posibles conocimientos adquiridos durante la intervención.

The questionnaire contains the following questions:

1. Where do we primarily have our sexuality?
2. What are the parts of the male reproductive system (male genitalia)?
3. What are parts of the female reproductive system (female genital)?

4. How long does the menstrual cycle last approximately?
5. How many months does a pregnancy take?
6. What are birth control methods?
7. What are sexually transmitted diseases or STDs?
8. What is homosexuality?

3.1. Procedure

Step 1: Implementation of Screening Questionnaire for Sexual Education Needs

The following questionnaire was applied for the deaf in the enter of attention of people with disabilities with the goal of designing an education program based on the needs identified in the questionnaire.

During this process we received support from the team of sign language interpreters from the center of attention, who collaborated in the implementation of the questionnaire, working together to achieve our goals.

Step 2: Preparation of the Sex Education Program

The sex education program was developed from the proposals of several authors (Baen, 1973, Burt, 1976, Lopez, 1990, 2002) on sex education programs, with specific objectives, issues that cover the information needs identified in our sample.

In addition, we developed the program taking into account the specific characteristics and special needs of our group.

3rd Step: Intervention

Intervention was applied in the Sexual Education Program for the Deaf from the center of attention of people with disabilities in one of its rooms, with a total duration of 5 hours. Throughout the course, we had the important role of one of the interpreters of Spanish Sign Language, who formed an important part of this project. The supporting material that was used during the course were: Plates (transparencies) with sketches, drawings and photographs that enabled us to clarify some concepts and ideas and support material (for each participant) containing: Abstract of Sexual Education Program, sexual dictionary and sexual colloquial vocabulary.

Sex Education Program

The following table describes the contents of the program.

Table 2. Sex education program

Introduction	Constitution of Sexuality • Psychological aspects. • Biological aspects. • Emotional Aspects. • Social Aspects.
1. Sexual Anatomy	a) Reproductive Systems • Male reproductive system • Organs • Functions • Female reprouctive system • Organs • Functions b) Changes undergone by our bodies during puberty • How these changes occur • Description of changes c) Menstruation • Description of the phases of the menstrual cycle • Days of the cycle • Some problems during menstruation • Discovering the peak of a woman's fertility d) The Human Sexual Response • Definition e) Ejaculation • Definition • Process f) Masturbation • Definition • Masturbation does not cause damage • Practice proper masturbation g) Sexual Dysfunctions • Definitions • Causes • Classification

2. Reproduction	a) Fecundation • Definition • Process b) Pregnancy Development • Stages of development in the mother • Stages of development in the embryo-fetus • Diagnosis of pregnancy • Symptoms during pregnancy • Disease that can affect pregnancy c) Delivery • Natural Chidlbirth • Description • Cesarean birth • Description • Alternative birth • Lactation d) Abortion • Definition • Types of abortion • Definitions e) Infertility • Definition f) Sterility • Definition
3. Contraception	a) Contraceptive Methods • Definition • Objectives b) Types of contraceptive methods • Natural Methods • Description • Types of Contraceptive Methods • Artificial Methods • Description • Classification

4. RESULTS

Through the screening questionnaire applied to each of the participants, some relevant data that occured in general, was the situation where our population is before carrying out Sex Education Program.

Table 3. Information obtained through the screening questionnaire of needs

Talks on Sexuality	• 1 person has never received any information about sexuality • 11 have received information about sexuality o from friends o 5 from parents o from teachers • people want their future children receive sex education Members of this group want their future children receive sex education from: o Parents o Teachers o Experienced professionals
Subjects you have interest in	• Issues of sexuality that the group wanted people to know better: (from most to least selected) 1 Friendship, attraction, affection, warmth, love 2 Sexually Transmitted Diseases. 3 Contraceptive Methods • The issues of sexuality that most of them talked about with friends are: 1 Friendship, attraction, affection, warmth and love 2 Human Body 3 Sexually Transmitted Diseases 4 Sexual Desire
Request information about sexuality issues	• When you have any questions on any topic related to sexuality primarily seeking information, you go to: 1 A friend or relative 2 A person from the association.
Ask for support and guidance on issues of sexuality	• If you had a difficult situation,such as an unexpected pregnancy or a sexually transmitted disease, you would turn for help to 1st. A doctor 2nd. Relative 3rd. Some professional from the attention center for people with disabilities.

Some questions raised during the course are:

Table 4. Questions raised during the Sex Education Program

Sexual Anatomy	Balls (testicles) can break in an accident or illness?
Menstruation	How I can know my menstrual cycle? How I can know when to get pregnant?
Masturbation	The man can masturbate all day (24 hours)? Masturbation can affect our minds?
Fecundation	Why can't a second sperm enter an egg, why just one? What happens when two sperm, go to two ovaries and face two eggs? Why sometimes instead of being one fetus, they are 2 or 3 fetuses?
Pregnancy Development	How long is the fetus while it is small? Why do thin women vomit during pregnancy, and fat women do not? What happens to the stomach when the woman is pregnant, where does the stomach go?
Delivery	Why do some people have cesarean delivery? How big is the incision of cesarean delivery? What happens to the umbilical cord when the baby is born?
Lactation	A woman with cancer can breastfeed her baby? How long a mother can produce milk? When the baby is in utero, does it need to urinate and defecate?
Abortion	When do people take the abortion pill? What is the name of the pill for abortion?
Contraceptive Methods	What are the most effective contraceptive methods? Does the cervical mucus is like mucus from our nose? What is the rhythm method? What if there is no space is left as a deposit on a condom? What happens to the egg when there is ligation of fallopian tubes? Tubal ligation can cause a disease? The most effective method of contraception are oral contraceptives? Every day, women leave a large amount of vaginal discharge? The condom is the most effective contraceptive method?

Through all of this information obtained, we could identify various needs so that we can summarize that:

1. There is a need for sexual education talks by parents, as only five people in the group have had discussions about sexuality from their parents. We believe that differences in language between parents and children may be the major factor influencing poor communication on sexuality issues, as none of the parents know sign language to communicate with their deaf children.
2. It is necessary to enrich the knowledge of people in the group on the theme of friendship, attraction, affection, warmth and love; it is chosen as the theme that they would most like to know better and also match the theme they talk the most about with their friends.
3. It is necessary to develop and / or improve communication and dialogue between parents and deaf children on sexuality issues to build confidence of the children to talk to parents about difficult situations should they occur
4. Literature is needed on issues of sexuality, adapted to the needs of hearing impaired readers. Using a practical and simple language, with clear definitions, films and photographs to enhance the reader's understanding and leave them a clearer idea of using visual media.
5. It is necessary to know the facilities and services that provide information and guidance on issues of sexuality, as well as to learn to ask for specific help and information.

After the second application of knowledge assessment questionnaire of the group (the first application before taking any action and the second thereafter), compared the results of both questionnaires and note that in the initial questionnaire 86.6% of respondents are correct, while in the final questionnaire, 94.7% of the answers are correct, based on these results we can say that the difference between percentages is significant.

During our intervention through sexual education program showed:

1. The group showed much interest in the topics discussed with special attention to the exhibition in pictures, in the shell or in the written material and participating through formulated questions and comments about the topics discussed.
2. Most of the time the group remained in order, respecting the time of exposure. However, at times some students held simultaneous

interventions without taking turns that prevented understanding of the ideas they wished to communicate., They find it difficult to realize that another person is engaged in the same time, so that we can say that simultaneous participation at any time could be regarded as a lack of respect for other students.

3. The course had an absolute respect for the topics discussed among people in the group.
4. The course was conducted in a climate of trust through which students could participate without inhibition and without fear of criticism or ridicule by their comments or questions.

Conclusions

Throughout our work we found very interesting data, from which we elaborate some conclusions. The focus of people with disabilities expressed much interest in the integration of persons with disabilities and one of the areas of current interest is to provide opportunities to improve their knowledge in the field of sexuality.

Resistance identified in some professional help centers through some negative attitudes limited our work. For example, reluctant attitude to the program, uncooperative attitude, attitudes toward disqualifying it and the attitudes of intervention.

At home, seven people in our sample are communicated through oral language, five are reported by combining speech and sign language and two in home communicate through natural gestures.

This indicates that although the people in the group know sign language, they do not use it to communicate at home and this may be a limiting factor (lack of a common language between parents and children well-developed) that can lead to situations like we observe in the group: only five people have had discussions about sexuality from their parents and one person in the group that has 22 years old never received a talk about sexuality.

There is a need and demand for literature and other media on sexuality issues tailored to the needs of people with hearing impairment.

Only two people claim to understand any text they read and only nine people depending on the text reading.

The issues of sexuality that lead to more interest to the group are love, affection, attraction, warmth and friendship, sexual transmitted diseases and contraceptive methods. The subject of sexuality that causes less interest to members is sexual identity.

The deaf person immersed in their multiple barriers to communication is seriously affected in their sexual life, drawing from an early age a host of unresolved questions and concerns that result in isolation or fear of the sexuality issues.

While completing this work, we detected some excessive modesty in participants to discuss issues of sexuality that were declined or disappeared along our course. This makes us reflect and conclude that the lack of knowledge may prevent a healthy and balanced development of their sexual lives and limiting their opportunities to seek and find a partner.

REFERENCES

Baen, A. (1973). *Método práctico de Educación Sexual Colectiva*. Ed. Fontanella, Madrid.

Burt, J. (1976). *Educación Sexual*. Interamericana, México, 2ª Edición.

Campo, M. y Sánchez, A. (2003). La mujer con lesión medular: sexualidad y maternidad. *Terapia Sexual y de Pareja*, Vol. 16, pp. 4-18

Casado, R. (2001). E*ducación para la salud de jóvenes con discapacidad intelectual.* Ed. Servicio de Publicaciones. Universidad de Burgos, Burgos.

CNSE. (2003). *Glosarios 13. Salud: Sexualidad*. Fundación CNSE, Madrid.

Colin, D. (1985). *Psicología del niño sordo*. París: Masson, S. A.

Estébanez-Díaz, E., Salvador, D. M., Serna, J. M., Vázquez, A. M., Ferrer, C. J. y Valmaseda, M. (1996). *Las personas sordas y su realidad social.* Ministerio de Educación y Ciencia, Madrid.

Estrada, B. (2003). *Sordera, Salud mental y Género*. Memoria de Investigación no publicada. Universidad Pontificia de Salamanca.

Estrada, B. (2009). *Abuso sexual en niños y niñas sordas*. En: “Abuso sexual Infantil”. Argentina: Editorial Vergara.

Fernández-Viader, M. P. (1996). *La comunicación de los niños sordos: interacción comunicativa padres-hijos*. Promociones y publicaciones Universitarias, S.A., Barcelona.

Fernández-Mostaza, E. (2003). *El proceso de resocialización de los padres oyentes con hijos sordos*. En Cultura y Educación, 15 (2), 149-164. Barcelona.

Giglioli, D. (1994). *La sessualità del sordo: aspetti comportamentali e clinico-terapeutici*. Centro italiano di studi e consulenza sessuale: Argenta.

Giglioli, D. (1999). *La sessualita del sordo*. Centro italiano di studi e consulenza sessuale.

Gómez Zapiain. (1999). *Sexualidad y Afectividad en personas con Deficiencia.* Breve guía para la reflexión. Ponencia presentada en las Jornadas Formativas sobre personas con Discapacidad, Organizadas por la gerencia Territorial de Servicios Sociales y la Universidad de Burgos. Burgos, 21 y 22 de octubre.

Kyle, J. y Sutherland, H. (1990-1993). *Deaf children at home*. Project report. Centre of deaf studies, Bristo.

López- Ibor, J.M. (1981). *El libro de la Salud Sexual*. Ed. Uve, Madrid.

López, F. (1984). *Principios Básicos de la Educación Sexual*. Ed. Instituto de Ciencias de la Educación, Universidad de Salamanca, Salamanca.

López, F. (1990). *Educación Sexual.* Fundación Universidad- Empresa, Madrid.

López, F. (2002). *Sexo y afecto en personas con discapacidad.* Biblioteca Nueva, Madrid.

M. E. C. (1991). *Las necesidades Educativas Especiales del niño con Deficiencia Auditiva.* Centro Nacional de Recursos para la Educación Especial, Madrid.

Marchesi, A. (1999). *Psicología de la comunidad sorda*. Confederación Nacional de Sordos de España, Madrid.

Masters, W. H., Johnson, V. E., Biggs, M. y Kolodny, R. (1982). *Manual de Sexualidad Humana*. Ed. Piramide, Madrid.

Morali, A. (1967). *Sociología de las Relaciones Sexuales*. Ed. Iberoamericana, Madrid.

Moreno, A. (2000). *La Comunidad Sorda: Aspectos Psicológicos y Sociológicos*. Fundación CNSE, Madrid.

Myklebust, H. R. (1964). *The Psychology of deafness. Grune and Stratton.* Traducción castellana: Psicología del sordo. Versión castellana de la 2ª edición inglesa, 4ª impresión. (1971) Magisterio Español, Madrid.

National Child Traumatic Stress Network (2006). *White paper on addressing the trauma treatment needs of children who are deaf or hard of hearing and the hearing children of deaf parents.* Los Angeles, Calif., and Durham, NC: National Child Traumatic Stress Network, 2006, www.NCTSN.org.

National Institute on Deafness and Other Communication Disorders. (2005). Statistics about hearing disorders, ear infections, and deafness. Retrieved

May 5, 2005, from http://www.nidcd.nih.gov/health/ statistics/ hearing. asp#1

Nordqvist, I. (1991). S*exualidad y Discapacidad. Un tema que nos concierne a todos*. Ministerio de Asuntos Sociales. INSERSO, Madrid.

ONU. (1983). *Programa de Acción Mundial para las Personas con Discapacidad y Normas uniformes sobre la igualdad de oportunidades para las personas con Discapacidad*. Real Patronato de Prevención y de Atención a Personas con Minusvalía, Madrid.

Padden, C., and Humphries, T. (1988). *Deaf in America: Voices from a culture*. Cambridge, MA: Harvard University Press.

Pinedo, F. J. (1981). *El Sordo y su Mundo*. Fundación CNSE, Madrid.

Sánchez, A. y De Pinto, A. (2000). *Lesión Medular: Sexualidad y Fertilidad*. Ed. Global Pharma Press, Madrid.□□□□□□

Sullivan, P. M., Vernon, M., and Scanlan, J. (1987). Sexual abuse of deaf youth. *American Annals of the Deaf*, 132 (4), 256-262.

Traxler, C. B. (2000). The Stanford Achievement Test, 9th Edition: National norming and performance standards for deaf and hard-of-hearing students. *Journal of Deaf Studies and Deaf Education*, 5(4), 337-348.

Valmaseda, M., Sánchez, A., Gómez, L. y Díaz- Estébanez, E. (1991). *Las necesidades educativas especiales del niño con deficiencias auditivas.*

Valmaseda, M. (1995). Las personas con deficiencia auditiva. En M. A. Verdugo (Dir.). *Personas con discapacidad. Perspectivas psicopedagógicas y rehabilitadoras* (pp. 223 -271).1ª Edición. Siglo XXI, Madrid.

Valmaseda, M. (2004). El desarrollo socio-emocional de los niños sordos. En Domínguez, A. B. y Alonso, B. P. *La educación de los alumnos sordos hoy. Perspectivas y respuestas educativas* (pp. 121-142). Aljibe, Málaga.

Watzlawick, P., Beavin, B. J. y Jackson, D. D. (1967). *Teoría de la Comunicación humana*. Herder, Barcelona.

Chapter 4

PERCEIVED STRESS IN PRELOCUTIVE PROFOUNDLY DEAF PEOPLE

Benito Estrada Aranda, Mónica González Ramírez and René Landero Hernández

ABSTRACT

In this paper, we present the adaptation of the Perceived Stress Scale (PSS) of Cohen (Cohen, Kamarck and Mermelstein, 1983) to the Mexican sign language to assess perceived stress in the prelocutive profoundly deaf population, Adaptation is performed using an adapted version for the general population and Landero Mexican González (2008). The adapted version of deaf people in Mexico has been called PSS-ASM and consists of two formats, a video in Mexican sign language and other writing where they appear only response options on a Likert scale. It was applied simultaneously to a sample of 38 prelocutive profoundly deaf people using sign language to communicate. The PSS-ASM fit is true to the original version about content is concerned. However, unlike the listener population, in this sample perceived stress is divided into two factors, one factor expression of stress and other stress management. The sample reported a media higher in the control factor, is also a significative but negative correlation between the factors, that is, greater control of stress, reduced expression of stressful stimuli are perceived in the persons of the sample. The perceived stress in deaf people of the sample is characterized by a greater perceived control of stressful stimuli but with a lower expression of the same, no differences were found with the results reported in samples of listeners in terms of increased perception stress.

INTRODUCTION

In recent decades, stress has been defined from various theoretical positions, such is the case of the transactional perspective, where stress is defined as a relationship between the individual and its environment, this being assessed by the subject as threatening or overwhelming of its resources and pose a danger to their well-being (Cohen, 2000, Lazarus and Folkman, 1984). That is, for the filing of the stress, people interpret it through what we think, experience or stimuli we face in our environment as a threat rather than a challenge. Thus, the perception of stress from this interactional theory is deeply mediated by our senses and our thoughts about the stimulus that we perceive as stressful.

Landero Gonzalez (2008) has explained that although there are different approaches to the study of stress, it can be considered as: 1) an individual's response (sympathetic activation, release of catecholamines or cortisol, anxiety, anger, etc.). In this case stress acts as the dependent variable, 2) a phenomenon of the external environment (painful stimulation, noise, discussions, etc..), in this case the stress is considered an independent variable, and 3) an interaction (transaction) between the individual and the environment (as process) (Sandin, 1999).

Thus, the study of stress in Deaf[1] people acquires special interest because this interaction is mediated by a purely visual perception, the lack of auditory perception and the use of a media visuospatial as is the sign language. In this regard and in line with the interactional perspective of stress (Cohen, 2000, Lazarus and Folkman, 1984), it is very interesting to question whether the evaluation / interpretation thatDeaf people can get to make as stressful stimuli is mediated or not for lack of a large cluster of auditory information, essential in the cognitive assessment conducted by interpreting an event.

[1] In this paper when referring to Deaf people with "D" capitalized, we will refer to the group of people born profoundly deaf, who use the SL to communicate and have a sense of belonging to the deaf community, as a collective population distinct from the rest, with a distinctive culture and contact with reality (call it social, family, work, education) merely visual.

It is also interesting to contemplate that the focus of the transactional theory is the cognitive evaluation we make about the events that we are stressed and in the case of Deaf people, because the cognitive processing may be compromised or delayed if the deaf child does not develop a system of communication, whether oral or sign language, the cognitive assessment may not be the same way as we would the listeners. For Torres (1999), learning the first language is the first cognitive feat carried out by the human subject. In the case of deaf children, learning the first language is double feat when learning a communication code with double representation: the spoken language and sign language (Estrada, 2008b). Through language, humans develop our cognitive functions and even for sign language (Grosjean, 1994). Thus, this reflection on language and its role in the development of cognitive functions and skills is of utmost importance to understand that stress Deaf people who use sign language to communicate can perceive and evaluate according to their cognitive development.

Traditionally, in the case of deaf children to study the implications of delay in oral language acquisition has been the focus of study since the middle of the last century. For example, Furth (1966) studied Deaf people in researches on the role of language in thought and reached the following conclusions: a) No such test can be used to correctly measure verbal intelligence in speech-impaired individuals, most of these tests are based on language skills and therefore do not give us the pattern of cognitive fitness, b) intelligence tests have been thinking of a certain type of people which are not part of the deaf, c) the environment influences on language. Hence the importance of assessing Deaf people from the most competitive language of communication, that is sign language. The majority of prelocutive profoundly deaf people who did not receive oral education and living in families of listeners, use sign language as their first or only form of communication.

Although these findings were made several decades ago, they are still valid in the sense that even the number of diagnostic instruments and tests, both intelligence as other skills or areas of development to evaluate or diagnose Deaf people are still very low or almost zero, especially in Mexico. This situation has conditioned and largely limited research with the group of Deaf people.

Finally, Estrada (2008b) brought together the main conclusions Furth (1966) found, in particular would be that the cognitive development of deaf children is similar to the listeners reaching the period of formal operations. He also notes that as a direct result of linguistic incompetence, deaf people fail or have poor performance on tasks that are specifically verbal. The evidence of conceptual thinking in the Deaf person takes Furth to the conclusion that thinking develops through contact with the environment, whether or not a system of linguistic symbols. Marchesi (1987) mentioned that Furth, deafness is not necessarily connected with the lack of intelligence. However, considering that language is not essential for the development of Deaf people, it was thought it had some effects that could be considered as negative (Balmaseda, 1995).

In abstract, these findings suggest that the cognitive development of profoundly deaf people in general will be slow and laborious manifested mainly in the following skills (Marchesi, 1999): 1 .- the ability to plan and anticipate the behavior situations. 2 .- the capacity to receive information and to expand the general knowledge about reality and 3 .- the ability to hypothesize and reason about various alternatives mentally. Although it concludes, Marchesi also states that "the deaf have an intellectual capacity equal to that of the listeners. However, faced with two problems arising from hearing impairment and are very closely related: the difficulty of acquiring oral language and the difficulty to extend the information and knowledge. Both limitations can be overcome through the acquisition and use of sign language "(p.33).

1. Stress and Deaf Adults

In other works, Gonzalez and Landero (2008) have studied the current fields of psychology of stress, referring to the term not as a sub-discipline of psychology, but rather to point out that stress should be tackled from all fields of psychology. Derived from the study of these authors, we conclude that the stress has been studied relatively little in people with disabilities in general and, in particular, the deaf.

A first impression might be thought that stress correlates with hearing loss and they have also identified other authors (Jones, Ouellette and Joungmi, 2006). However, there are still no studies that provide preliminary data that confirm or rule it out. In this vein, Jones, and Joungmi Ouellette (2006) explain that it is logical to assume that most Deaf people experience the same range of stressors experienced by hearing people. Although distinct from their perspectivein the case of the experience of Deaf people, it is likely that some particular conditions they face increase the risk of stress, such is the case of unemployment, underemployment, difficulties arising from the daily interaction with the "hearing world"; scenarios that are very accessible communicationally speaking, and stress from the experience of being part of a minority culture in the social and linguistical, thus encouraging a breach of human rights (Estrada, 2008b).

They also point out that in looking at the findings of Cohen and Williamson's (1988) on stress, one can identify a considerable number of potential stressors which may be subjects for deaf adults, for example, socioeconomic status, unemployment and sub-employment, work in occupations that are seen with a low social status, and membership of an ethnic minority group.

2. Statistics on Stress, Mental Health and Deafness in Mexico

In Mexico, official figures have not informed us about the incidence of psychological disorders in the Mexican deaf people, including anxiety disorders and stress. The National Psychiatric Epidemiology Survey (NPES) carried out between 2001 and 2002, is the first and only national statistical reference about the mental health status of Mexicans. However, it provides no evidence on the mental health of deaf people, or for any person with a disability because of the 8.826 respondents they do not know if any of them had a disability. What is interesting is the fact that this survey found that anxiety disorders are more prevalent and more chronic, while more prevalent individual disorders were major depression, specific phobia, social phobia and alcohol dependence. Unfortunately, we do not know if this occurs also among the deaf.

The most surprising result in the general population of Mexican listeners is that only one in 10 people with a mental disorder received treatment and only one in 10 with three or more disorders received care. In conclusion, the NPES is clear that the mental health assessment of people with disabilities is not taken into account sot therefore we do not know how many people with disabilities are receiving care for a mental disorder.

We believe that anxiety disorders may be affecting Deaf people more than they affect hearing people, but there are some basic problems that currently prevent checking. On the one hand, the majority of Deaf people with a mental health problem do not go to a mental health professional to seek help (at least in Mexico and in most countries), and on the other hand, there is an absence of official statistics on mental health of people with disabilities in general, and particularly of the deaf community.

As an example, Estrada (2008a) mentioned that the only public service for mental health and deafness for the deaf in Spain[2] aims to provide specific treatment to Deaf people, the most common diagnoses have been made are the anxiety disorders and conduct disorders (Garcia, 2003).

It is of utmost importance to gain access to an objective assessment, specific and comprehensive mental health problems in the general population in Mexico and in particular to Deaf people. We say it is especially important with Deaf people because, of the wide variety of disabilities, deafness is the one that offers more complex barriers and is more difficult to avoid in the context of mental health and deafness as we talk about communication barriers. In Mexico, the vast majority of mental health professionals do not know sign language and most of them would be unable to carry out a mental health evaluation and subsequent treatment of deaf people using mexican sign language to communicate. The right to health protectionis one more of the human rights of deaf people which are violated in Mexico., (Estrada, 2008b).

3. Cultural Identity and Stress

Deaf deep people who were born deaf or who lost hearing before early childhood (prelocutive deafness) are born mostly in families with parents and hearing members (Marchesi, 1999). This reality leads to the deaf person seeking interaction and integration with other deaf people with whom to communicate and to bond, thus arises the deaf community and also the so-called "deaf identity" (Kyle, 1990). Padden and Humphries (1984) pointed out that the deaf have their own culture because they share a language (sign language), a history / experience as a deaf person, experiences in common with the hearing society and a strong and sustainable social network . Estébanez Diaz et al., (1996) explain that the recognition of the collective deaf as a social group with specific characteristics is based largely on the idea that the connection to the world through the vision and the use of a sign language conferring own identity issues. In addition, Deaf people that make up the deaf community, are perceived as a distinct social group (Rodríguez, Maple and Sabucedo, 1997) and as members of a group that identifies and where they are

[2] Hospital Gregorio Marañón, Madrid (Spain).

comfortable. (Kyle, 1990). Even Lane (2005) defines Deaf people as an ethnic group since they have a collective name, feelings of belonging to the community, standards of behavior, distinct values, knowledge (of their own culture), customs, social structure, language own art and history. Other authors (Glikman, 1993) have developed theories about the development of deaf identity, noting that some listeners construct an identity, marginal, bicultural, and finally immersed. This is where stress can begin to have relationship with each of these identities, as each one of them conducive frameworks of interaction, integration and communication are distinct. Unfortunately, it has not been sufficiently explored the relationship between cultural identity and stress in Deaf people, which represents an area of opportunity for research. In the first chapter of this book, it refers to the cultural identity of theDeaf, explaining that the theory of Deaf Identity Development, known as DIDT, proposed by Glickman (1993) consists of four identities: culturally listener, culturally marginal, culturally immersed and bicultural identity. Following this theory (DIDT), Leigh and Pollard (2003) have found that deaf adults with marginal cultural identities (which means, that are not identified with the deaf community or with the hearing community) have more difficulty adapting. In this sense, we think it is very likely that this difficulty in generating adaptation of anxiety and stress, with a greater perception of maladjustment, the less well perceived. For some authors, the difference between deaf and hearing people is not that one can hear and the other can not, but on the cultural consequences that it causes (Balmaseda, 1995). This implies that the impact of stress may be different for each person according to Deaf cultural identity which predominates, according to Glickman's theory (1993) above. For Estrada (2008a), the construction of cultural identity is very interesting and important not only because it reflects in relation to the construction of the identity of Deaf people as has been studied by Glickman (1993), but because through it proposes an identity of Deaf people that can be far more constructive and sociocultural, away from deficit or pathology.

4. Stress in Hearing Family with a Deaf Member

Some authors (Marschark, 1993; Marchesi, 1999) indicate that over 90% of profoundly deaf children are born into hearing families. This means that only between 5% and 10% of deaf children have deaf parents. This reality has a profound impact on the parental bond, this is in the relationship and the dynamics that parents establish with their children, and will be completely different if both have the same communication system. It is not the same for a hearing mother to speak fluent with her son when he has a bad conduct or when to call her attention that a hearing mother with a deaf child with which basic questions can only be told by natural signs, things like a simple "no." In the first case, the listener mother has the opportunity to explain to her child why they must not behave that way, and that is in many ways a way to channel the stress generated by the child's misbehavior. In the case of the listener mother of a deaf child, this explanation can hardly be because most hearing parents of deaf children do not learn sign language. In contrast, the deaf parents with deaf children, teach their children sign language as their first language, these children seem to have a more on par with the development of hearing children with hearing parents. Authors such as Dominguez and Alonso (2004), explain that in the previous investigation, it seems to be consensus to say in conclusion that deaf children exposed to sign language in their family and at an early age, they acquire the language at a rate maturing identical to how hearing children acquire spoken language, especially when the deaf child is the son of deaf parents. The process of acquisition of sign language by deaf children remains with undeniable similarities with the development of spoken language by hearing children (Torres et al., 1995). On the other hand, ithas been found that deaf children of deaf parents are relatively more mature than deaf children of hearing parent.(Meadow, 1980). The deaf parents and children maintain the same language (sign language) and greatly influences the development of psychic structure in the development of healthy self-esteem, building a positive self-concept and the development of a healthy deaf identity. These Deaf parents relate to their child naturally through sign language, children identify with their deaf parents and grow within the same community, the deaf community. In addition, deaf children of deaf parents, grow up in a cultural, socio-cultural and communicative very different, thus increasing the quality and quantity of their social skills, facilitating their socio-emotional development and identity formation (Estrada , 2008a). However, for hearing parents with deaf children there are many complications in establishing a bond and the deaf child will present a delay in oral language acquisition, including, in many cases, neither parents nor the child learn sign language early (before the first five years), keeping both without an effective means of communication to establish a parental relationship and a strong identification with parental figures. Over time, these children grow up with the constant search for social identification, such as deaf or hearing, resulting in the development of cultural identity. On the other hand, several studies indicate the presence of psychosocial stress in hearing parents of deaf children (Burger,

Spahn, Richter, Eissele, et al., 2005). In families where there is a deaf member, stress is not just for hearing parents, but for the rest of the family as well (Hinterm and Horsch, 1998). Basically, the confrontation between family members in relation to the family's deafness makes differences arise between them; feelings, disagreements, hopelessness and aggression (Wunsch and Bengel, 1998). Other studies have reported that there is no clinically significant difference between levels of stress in mothers of deaf children and mothers of hearing children (Pipp, Sedey and Yoshinaga, 2002). However, Quittner (1991) finds differences between parents of hearing children and parents of deaf children in terms of parental stress levels. In other studies, (Estrada, 2008a) have explained how some authors (Myers, Myers and Marcus, 1999) have described two practical models for understanding the intrafamiliar dynamics of both families with hearing parents and deaf children as with deaf parents and hearing children. The first is a systemic model (Harvey, 1989), which focuses on the family to review and interpret the systemic and cultural context and family dynamics between deaf and hearing members. On the other hand, the second model (Thurman, 1985) focuses on the process between the family and the external environment. For Myers, Myers and Marcus (1999), this model is valuable because it has three dimensions in its structure that can be applied to hearing children of deaf parents and family: distance (as is seen by the family and the other members of the deaf child's ability to hear), competition (as the ability of hearing child helps to inform members of environmental sounds deaf or play the role of interpreter) and tolerance of differences (of the hearing child to deaf parents and vice versa, and how it fits into the family system of the child's ability to hear). For these families, Myers, Myers and Marcus (1999) suggest that therapists should find ways to promote and encourage the family in a way that promotes communication and interaction, educating deaf members about "listener culture" and the hearing members about the "deaf culture."

5. The Assessment of Perceived Stress in Deaf People

To evaluate the stress (in general, psychological variables) perceived in Deaf people using sign language to communicate poses several challenges. The first is to assess from the language of mayor competition from deep prelocutive Deaf people: sign language, which implies a translation of an oral-written language to a manual-visual-spatial (due to the space component of hands). The second is to ensure that they understand what is being evaluated, in this sense we speak of adaptations culturally valid (Brauer, 1989, 1993) if in addition to ensuring the translation (usually using the back translation procedure), are working to adapt items in that are understood by Deaf people without changing the intent of the assessment or order of the item. The third challenge, once again exceeded the previous ones, is to ensure the validity of the assessment. Finally, the greatest of all challenges is that Deaf people understand the items (in terms of understanding cognitive concerns) so we can assess the construct we are measuring accurately. Stress has become in recent years perhaps the most studied variable in health psychology, the result of years of research has shown its negative impact on health. For example, we studied the relationship between stress and cardiovascular problems in the general population (Cohen, Kaplan, and Manuck, 1994; Linden, Stossel, and Maurice, 1996; Ryff and Singer, 1998) and for the first time in deaf people in an educational program for primary prevention (Heart Health Intervention; DHHI), coronary heart disease for the Deaf (Jones, Oullette and Kang, 2006). It is in this last study, where perceived stress was assessed by the Perceived Stress Scale (PSS, Cohen et al., 1983; Cohen, Kaplan, and Manuck, 1994) using a version of the PSS of 10 items. In this chapter, we report the application of PSS for the first time in prelocutive profoundly deaf people in Mexico, using the Mexican version of PSS validated for general mexican listener population (González and Landero, 2007). Jones, Ouellette and Kang (2006) have reported data using a version of the PSS of 10 items (Cohen et al., 1983; Cohen, Kaplan, and Manuck, 1994) in Deaf people and is perhaps the first study to provide such data. This study is actually a design study with a control group and an experimental group aimed at obtaining experimental data on the effectiveness of cognitive-behavioral intervention as a treatment for stress in a sample of 104 Deaf people (the authors do not report accurately whether it is of prelocutive profoundly deaf). There was an average score of 17.65 in the experimental group and 14.29 in the control group before treatment. This study concludes that some Deaf adults may experience higher levels of perceived stress than the general population listener.

6. THE PERCEIVED STRESS IN PROFOUNDLY PRELOCUTIVE MEXICAN DEAF

To measure perceived stress in prelocutive profoundly deaf people in Mexico, used was the Perceived Stress Scale, PSS-Cohen (Cohen, Kamarck and Mermelstein, 1983), in adapting to Mexico by Gonzalez and Landero (2008). The PSS consists in 14 questions, never scores -0 - very often -4 -. Reversing the score in the seven negative items, the highest score corresponds to greater perceived stress. The version that was taken as the basis for sign language translation, obtained an alpha of .83 in a sample of Mexican students (González and Landero, 2007), and reflect the two factors reported in the original version of Cohen and Williamson (1988), grouping the items themselves forward and reverse respectively. To qualify, you must reverse the negative items, which are those that assess stress management (negative items: 4, 5, 6, 7, 9, 10 and 13). It uses an adapted version of the PSS to the Mexican Sign Language for Deaf people which was called prelocutive profound PSS-ASM (adapted to Mexican Deaf) which was adapted from the version of Gonzalez and Landero (2007) in Mexico, this version has been adapted in this study following the procedure known as reverse translation which has been described elsewhere (Estrada, 2009). The PSS-ASM consists of two formats, which includes only one written response option on a Likert scale and the other in a visual format, where there is a Deaf person signing The instructions and 14 items of the instrument with response options . The application form is to use both formats simultaneously, the video for Deaf people can be assessed in their language, and writing, so they can make the answer to every question.

The PSS-ASM was applied in a secondary school with two groups of Deaf people who are fluent in mexican sign language. We used a 25-minute session with each group in charge of implementation was an listener interpreter of mexican sign language. The first phase of adaptation was to ascertain whether the scale measures what it should measure (that is, whether it is valid also in deaf people using mexican sign language to communicate) and if its questions are interrelated enough to measure stress (this is, if there is reliability of internal consistency). Thus, to verify that the scale measures what it should measure was performed reverse translation process what was evidence of content validity, experts say, the scale has the content needed to measure stress and this version is equivalent to listeners version adapted to Mexico. To assess reliability, we used the Cronbach alpha coefficient, which assesses the internal consistency precisely. What we expected to find was that the 14 items forming the scale were sufficiently interrelated to work with a single score of perceived stress. However, in the sample where the PSS was applied, considering the 14 items as one scale did not provide a good internal consistency, indicating that the items are not summable in a single score that reflects perceived stress in this sample of Deaf people. For this reason, we decided to assess the internal consistency of each of the two factors that have been reported in various studies of PSS with versions in English (Cohen and Williamson, 1988), Spanish for Mexico (González and Landero, 2007) and Japanese (Mimura and Griffiths, 2008).

Table 1. Measures of central tendency and dispersion for both factors

	Median	Average	Standard Deviation
Stress expression	10.0	10.4	6.2
Stress management	14.0	15.7	7.2

Scale was divided into positive and negative items (7 for each subscale), this division showed good internal consistency for both subscales: α =. 84 for positive items and α =. 85 for negative items, all items correlated well in the corresponding subscale.

Thus, for the sample of deaf people in contrast to what was reported in previous literature with the PSS, is considered appropriate to consider two separate scores, one expression of stress (positive items) and a control (reverse items) of stress. The term stress refers exclusively cognitive and stress management concerns to have dealt adequately with stressful situations. With these, two scores of these tests are performed to explore the level of perceived stress to the deaf.

There was a negative correlation between expression of stress and stress management (r = -763, p =. 001), which means that the higher the expression of stress scores, lower scores on stress management. Comparing men and women found no significant difference (expression of stress: t = -. 310, p =. 758; stress control: t = 0.079, p =. 938).

To determine if these scores reflect high or low levels, the ideal would be to compare scores with other samples of hearing people. However, the PSS is usually analyzed in a single score, so scores are not available for the expression of stress and stress management separately from other investigations and that, while not the most advisable way was considered that the route of the scale had changed, with the original 0-56 for each factor is 0 to 28, so it is divided by 2 the average PSS reported in other samples and compared with the expression of stress in the sample of deaf (is considered a better indicator of stress than the control factor).

Thus, we find that the expression of stress of the sample is not very distant from the estimate for students, but lower than in chronic diseases like diabetes and fibromyalgia.

Table 2. Comparison between samples where the PSS has been applied

	Estimated score for expression of stress (average/2)	Raw Scores of PSS		
		Median	Average	SD
Deaf	10.36	---	---	---
EB	10.85	23.00	21.7	6.54
Diabetes	19.05	---	38.1	14.35
Heart Disease	13.95	25.00	27.9	8.9
HIV	11.3	---	22.6	8.67
Fibromyalgia	15.15	31	30.3	9.91
Cancer	8.77	---	17.55	6.72
Students	10.95	21	21.9	4.07

Sources: EB: Reyna (2009), Diabetes: Salazar and Lozano (2006), Heart disease: Channels (2009), HIV: Remor and Carrobles (2001) Fibromyalgia: González, García-Campayo and Landero (2008), Students: González and Landero (2008).

These results mean, unlike what happens in hearing people, that the sample of Deaf people in this study, items measuring the expression of stress and stress management can not join it because there is no consistency internal, this is not related enough to say that measure a single variable, which in this case, is the perceived stress. This means that the assessment of perceived stress using the PSS-ASM Deaf, is measured in terms of the expression of stress and perceived control with stress (this is, with two factors and not just one, as would in listener population).

However, the average stress management factor is higher than in the expression of stress, indicating that the Deaf people sample perceive stressful stimuli control more than they express. This result is consistent with the negative correlation found between the expression of stress and stress management, this is a greater perception of stress management, lower expression of perceived stress.

No significant relationship was found either with age or sex and there are no significant gender differences. Finally, we find that the expression of the stress of the sample is not very distant from the estimate for students, but lower than in patients with chronic diseases like diabetes and fibromyalgia.

7. Treatment of Stress on the Deaf People

Like other mental health problems such as depression (Estrada, 2008a), stress treatment in the Deaf population has been a little studied and so far we have few reports of interventions with deaf patient samples, and in particular, we do not have that information in Mexico. Authors of one of these few studies (Jones, Ouellette and Kang, 2006) explain that although it is very common argument that deafness correlated positively with stress, it is empirically demonstrated in the literature, and so far, studies have examined the methods and techniques of intervention to deal with stress in Deaf people are very scarce. Although there is little research to help design specific treatments for Deaf people with stress, Leigh and Pollard (2003) explain that the previous literature suggests that most psychotherapeutic treatment is cognitive behavioral therapy which may benefit more Deaf people in general, and in particular, for the treatment of stress.

In the review Jones, Ouellette and Kang (2006) made on the issue of stress in Deaf people, it concluded that the previous empirical literature on this subject does not provide evidence of whether the perceived stress in adult Deaf people is different from what people perceive in the general listener population. However, because the Deaf people face more stressful situations resulting from the absence of the sense of hearing and communication barriers, at least in theory this makes us think that will lead to more situations of social interaction and communication barriers that could be a source of stressful stimuli in this population. In addition, mental health services and deafness are very little, if any, and there are few mental health professionals who know sign language and psychosocial variables, such as culture and language of the deaf population, so this makes the presence of these mental health problems in Deaf people higher and experienced little support. In Mexico, there is not a public mental health service specifically for Deaf people to be offered through Mexican sign language.

Cognitive behavioral treatment of stress, focuses on getting people to control our responses to cognitive stimuli that cause us anxiety, and stress. By controlling the way we think about what we are stressed of, we can learn to change our perception of the feeling of stress. Speaking of control, we refer to the parameters of intensity, frequency and duration of the stress response. This response may be through irrational or distorted thoughts, which tend to be intense and difficult to remove, but once changed, is the basis for behavioral and emotional change.

The only study that we report that has made a cognitive-behavioral intervention with deaf patients, is the study of Jones, Ouellette and Kang (2006). These authors designed an intervention program for primary prevention (coronary disease) unique for the Deaf called: The Deaf Heart Health Intervention (DHHI). In this study, a total of 104 Deaf people over 18 years, self-identified as members of the deaf community, and not had a diagnosis of coronary disease. The contents of DHHI (see also Table 3) consists of information on cardiovascular disease, heart healthy nutrition, physical activity and exercise, smoking cessation training and talks on managing stress and negative effects of stress on health. In the DHHI,the theoretical foundation is the social-cognitive theory of Bandura (1986, 1995), supplemented with research results on the main teaching-learning strategies for Deaf people (Eng, McKee, and Conner, 1993; Lang , Stinson, Basile, Kavanagh, and Uu, 1999) and knowledge of the lifestyles of Deaf people (Dolnick, 1993; Padden and Humphries, 1988), among others. The DHHI lasts a total of eight weeks, spread over a total of 16 hours. The content on stress and stress management consisted of relaxation techniques. Also, participants were trained in adapted form of cognitive restructuring in a way that is relevant to Deaf people. Thus, some examples of cognitive restructuring were related to frustrating situations involving interactions between deaf and hearing people in different contexts. The program also includes training in muscle relaxation and breathing. The study of Jones, Ouellette and Kang (2006) has a quasi-experimental design with an intervention in an experimental group and a control group receiving an alternative treatment for eight weeks only social recreation.

The authors of this study hypothesized that those who received DHHI intervention in the experimental group described in Table 3, perceive less stress than Deaf people in the control group who received no treatment. The way to know which of the two groups perceived less stress, was using a version of the PSS of 10 items (Cohen et al., 1983; Cohen, Kaplan, and Manuck, 1994) before and after the treatment. As in our study, the PSS was translated into sign language (in this case American Sign Language) and recorded on video, also using reverse translation procedure that we report (Jones, Lee, Phillips, Zhang, and Jaciedo, 2001). Although unlike the study of

Jones, Ouellette and Kang (2006), the PSS used in our study is of 14 items validated for the general Mexican listener population (González and Landero, 2007).

A limitation of this study is that participants were not randomly assigned to either group, this is because the deaf community, in the cities in which they conducted the studies, is relatively small. However, rather than a limitation, this represents a basic difficulty, since this is usually one of the problems we face when doing research with people who belong to minority groups such as Deaf people.

Table 3. Intervention program for deaf heart health. Objectives related to stress and coping with stress

Course participants will:
• Define stress. • Explain the effects of stress on long-term health. • Demonstrate the effects of deep breathing for relaxation. • Learn at least three strategies for coping with stress. • Setting targets for stress management using the five steps of change. • Identify ways to change thoughts about stressful situations. • Explain how friends and family can help in stressful situations. • Evaluate progress using goals of coping with stress. • Identify strategies to continue to conduct stress coping practices after the course of heart health.

As for the main results, we mention that we found a significant difference in PSS scores before and after treatment in the experimental group, compared with the control group. With this, it follows that the group of deaf people who received treatment, significantly reduced their perception of stress. The study also concludes that the majority of Deaf adults who suffer from stress have little access to information about stress management. In this study proves that when given a treatment adapted to the cultural needs (sign language) for Deaf people, they can benefit and learn skills to cope with stress.

Conclusions

The study of stress in profoundly deaf people is an issue that needs further investigationand is needed to confirm these results from the application of PSS-ASM to expand the sample. In this sense, the results reported in this paper are preliminary because the study is still underway to expand the sample. The perceived stress reported in eaf people sample is characterized by a greater perceived control of stressful stimuli but with a lower expression of the same. This is important information because it may help improve treatments for stress in eaf people emphasizing the expression of stressful stimuli in order to improve coping. No differences were found with the results reported in samples of listeners in terms of increased perception of stress.

References

Bandura, A. (1995). *Self-efficacy in changing societies.* New York; Cambridge University Press.

Bandura. A (1986), *Social foundations of thought and action: A social-cognitive theory.* Englewood Cliffs, NJ: Prentice Hall.

Brauer, B. (1989). *A translation of the MMPI into sign language for use in deaf individuals: an assessment of translation accuracy.* Manuscrito no publicado, Gallaudet University. Washington, DC.

Brauer, B. (1993). Adequacy of a translation of the MMPI into American Sign Language for use with deaf individuals: Linguistic equivalency issues. *Rehabilitation Psychology, 38,* 247-260.

Burger, T., Spahn, C., Richter, B., Eissele, S., Löhle, E., and Bengel, J. (2005). *Parental Distress: The Initial Phase of Hearing Aid and Cochlear Implant Fitting.* American Annals of the Deaf. 150, (1), pp. 5-10.

Canales, L. (2009). Intervención cognitivo-conductual para la disminución del estrés en pacientes con cardiopatía isquémica. Tesis de Maestría. Facultad de Psicología. UANL.

Cohen, J. I. (2000). Stress and mental health: A biobehavioral perspective. *Issues in Mental Health Nursing,* 21,185-202.

Cohen, S., and Williamson, M. (1988). *Perceived stress in a probability sample of the United States.* In S. Spacapan and S. Oscampc (Eds.), The social iwchvlofy of health (pp. 31-67). Newbury Park, CA: Sage.

Cohen, S., Kamarck, T., and Mermelstein, R. (1983). A global measure of perceived stress. *Journal of Health and Social Behavior*, 24, 385-396.

Cohen, S., KaplanJ. K., and Manuck, S. U. (1994). *Social support and coronary heart disease: Underlying psychologic and biologic mechanisms*. In S. A. Shumaker and S. M. Czajkowski (Eds.), Social support and cardiovascular disease (pp. 195-221). New York: Plenum Press.

Díaz-Estébanez, E., Salvador, D. M., Serna, J. M., Vázquez, A. M., Ferrer, C. J., Serna, M. J., Valmaseda, M. (1996). *Las personas Sordas y su realidad social. Un estudio descriptivo.* Ministerio de Educación y Ciencia: Madrid.

Dolnick, E. (1993, September). Deafness as a culture. *Atlantic Monthly,* pp. 37-53.

Domínguez, A. B y Alonso, B. P. (2004). *La educación de los alumnos sordos hoy. Perspectivas y respuestas educativas*. Aljibe: Málaga.

Eng, E., Parker, E., and Harlan, C. (1997). Lay health adviser intervention strategies: A continuum from natural helping to paraprofessional helping. *Health Education and Behavior,* 24(4), 413-17.

Estrada, A. B. (2008b). La vulneración de los derechos humanos de las personas Sordas en México. *Revista del Centro Nacional de Derechos Humanos*, 3, (8), pp. 105-127.

Estrada, B. (2008a). *Salud mental: depresión y sordera.* Monterrey, Nuevo León, México: Universidad Autónoma de Nuevo León.

Estrada, A. B. (2009). Metodología para la adaptación de instrumentos de evaluación psicológica a la lengua de señas mexicana. En: Moral, J, (Comp). Investigaciones en psicología social, personalidad y salud.

Furth, H. G. (1966). *Thinking without language: psychosocial implications of deafness.* New York. Free Press. Traducción castellana: *Pensamiento sin lenguaje. Implicaciones Psicológicas de la Sordera.* Madrid: Marova, 1981.

García, G, A. (2003). Comunicación presentada en las V Jornadas Científicas de Investigación sobre personas con discapacidad. 20-22 de marzo, Salamanca.

Glickman, N. (1993). *Deaf Identity Development: Construction and Validation of a Theoretical Model.* Tesis de doctorado no publicada, Universidad de Massachusetts.

González, M.T., and Landero, R. (2007). Factor Structure of the Perceived Stress Scale (PSS) in a Sample from Mexico. *The Spanish Journal of Psychology* (10) 1, 199-206.

González, M.T. and Landero, R. (2008). Confirmación de un modelo explicativo del estrés y de los síntomas psicosomáticos mediante ecuaciones estructurales. Revista Panamericana de Salud Pública, 23 (1), 7-18.

González, M.T., García-Campayo, J. and Landero, R. (2008). *The role of stress transactional theory on the development of fibromyalgia: A structural equation model, Artículo enviado para publicación.*

Grosjean, F. (1994). Sign bilingualism: Issues. In *The Encyclopedia* of *Language and Linguistics*. Oxford: Pergamon Perss.

Hintermair, M. and Horsch, U. (1998). Horschadigung als Kritisches Lebensereignis: Aspekte der Belastongund Bewaltingung von Eltern horgeschadigter Kinder, Heidelberg, Germany: Gross.

Jones, G. E., Ouellette, E.S., and Joungmi, K. (2006). Perceived stress among deaf adults. *American Annals of the deaf.* 151, (1), 25-31.

Jones, P S., U-e, J. W, Phillips, L. R., Zhang, X. E. *and* Jaciedo, K. B. (2001). An adaptation of Brislin's translation model for cross-cultural research. *Nursing Research* 50(5), 300-304.

Jones, P. S., Lee J. W, Phillips, I. R., Zhang, X. E., and Jaciedo, K. B. (2001). An adaptation of Brislin's translation model for cross-cultural research. Nursing Rent-arch 50(5), 300-304.

Kyle, J. (1990). The Deaf Community: Culture, Custom and Tradition. En S. Prillwitz y T. Vollhaber (eds.) *Sign Language Research and Application. Hamburg: Signum Press.*

Lane, H. (2005). Ethnicity, ethics, and the Deaf-World. *The Journal of Deaf Studies and Deaf Education, 10* (3), 291-310.

Lang, H. G., Stinson, M. S., Ba.sile, M., Kavanagh, F., and Liu, Y (1999). Learning styles of deaf college students and teaching behaviors of their instructors. *Journal of Deaf Studies and Deaf Education, 4,* 16-27.

Lazarus, R., and Folkman S. (1984). *Stress, coping and adaptation.* New York: Springer.

Leigh, 1. W, *and* Pollard, R. Q. (2003). Mental health and Deaf adults. In M. Marschark and P. Spencer (Eds.). *Deaf studies, language, and education* (pp. 190-202). Oxford, England: Oxford University Press.

Lozano, M. and Salazar, B. (2006). Estrés percibido y adaptación en pacientes con diabetes mellitus tipo 2. Revista ACHICAN, 7 (1), 77-84.

Marchesi, A. (1987). *El desarrollo cognitivo y lingüístico de los niños sordos.* Madrid: Alianza Psicología.

Marchesi, A. (1999). *Psicosociología de la comunidad Sorda.* Madrid: Confederación Nacional de Sordos de España.

Marschark, M. (1993). *Psychological Development of Deaf Children*. New York: Oxford University Press.

Meadow, K. P. (1980). *Deafness and child development*. London: Edward Arnold.

Mimura, Ch. and Griffiths, P. (2008). A Japanese version of the Perceived Stress Scale: cross-cultural translation and equivalence assessment. BMC Psychiatry, 8, 85 Article URL http://www.biomedcentral.com/1471-244X/8/85

Myers, S., Myers, R., y Marcus, A. (1999). Hearing Children of Deaf Parents : Issues and Interventions within a Bicultural Context. En W. I. Leigh (Ed.), *Psychotherapy with deaf clients from diverse groups* (pp. 121-148). Washington: Gallaudet University Press.

Padden, C., y Humphires, T. (1988). *Deaf in America: Voices from a culture.* Cambridge, MA: Harvard University Press.

Pipp-Siegel, S., Sedey, A. L., and Yoshinaga-Itano, C. (2002). Predictors of parental stress in mothers of young children with hearing loss. *Journal of Deaf Studies and Deaf Education*, 7, 1–17.

Quittner, A. C. (1991). Coping with a hearing-impaired child. In. J. H. Johnsoin and S. B. Johnson (Eds.). *Advances in child health psychology* (pp. 206-223). Gainsesville: University of Florida Press.

Remor, E. and Carrobles, J. (2001). Versión Española de la escala de estrés percibido (PSS-14): Estudio psicométrico en una muestra VIH+. Ansiedad y Estrés, 7 (2-3), 195-201.

Reyna, A. (2009). Psicodermatología: aspectos psicológicos en personas con epidermolisis bullosa. Tesis de Maestría. Facultad de Psicología. UANL.

Rodríguez, L., Arce, C., and Sabucedo J. (1997). Dimensiones de identidad social en jóvenes sordos. *Anuario de Psicología, Universitat de Barcelona, Vol. 72,* pp. 91-104.

Sandín, B. (1999). *Estrés psicosocial*. Madrid: Klinik.

Thurman, S. K. (1985). *Children of handicapped parents*. Orlando: Academic Press.

Torres, M. S. (1999). Lenguajes y cognición. En Torres, M., S., Urquiza de la Rosa, R., Santana, H., R. (1999) *Deficiencia Auditiva. Guía para profesionales y padres* (pp. 109-145). Málaga: Aljibe.

Torres, M., S., Rodríguez, S., J., Santana, H., R., González, C., A. (1995). *Deficiencia Auditiva. Aspectos psicoeducativos y educativos.* Málaga: Aljibe.

Valmaseda, M. (1995). La evaluación cognitiva de los niños y jóvenes sordos. *FIAPAS, 54,* 53-55.

Wunsch, A. and Bengel, J.(1998). Psychologische Aspekte von Körper- und Sinnesbehinderung. In: W. Molt (Hrsg): Handbuch der Angewandten Psychologie: Grundlagen - Methoden - Praxis. *Ecomed*, pp. 1-14.

Chapter 5

PROFILE AND INTENSITY OF DEPRESSION IN PRELOCUTIVE PROFOUNDLY DEAF PEOPLE IN MEXICO

Rosalinda Ruíz Ibarra and Benito Estrada Aranda

ABSTRACT

The theoretical review shows that there is agreement among authors regarding the increased vulnerability of the deaf population to psychological problems (Orihuela, Conde, Vargas, Martínez and Franco, 2000). Speaking specifically of enforcement, recent research has found higher rates of moderate and severe depression in deaf adolescents, youth and adults, as compared with their hearing peers (Leigh and Anthony, 2001; Estrada, Beyebach, Delgado and Freire, 2008). Research in Mexico has yielded similar results (Ruiz, 2009), finding a higher rate of moderate and severe depression when compared with other mexican listeners. We even detected the possibility of a depression profile different between deaf and hearing, because the deaf Mexicans have a higher number of somatic behavioral symptoms such as changes in appetite, tiredness, fatigue, loss of interest, crying, irritability, loss of energy and loss of interest in sex, when compared to Mexican listeners. All these findings invite us to reflect on the following questions: Why is this difference in symptomatic profile? Are deaf more concrete thinkers , to name a few.

Introduction

When starting the study of depression in deaf people, it is necessary to ask about the incidence and importance of this mood disorder. Currently, accurately estimating the incidence of depression in the general population in our country is a complex task. On the one hand, the number of people who self- diagnosed with depression or who have some depressive symptoms is surprisingly high. On the other hand, most of the statistics only take into account the number of people who come to seek help from a professional or health center (Vázquez and Sanz, 1991).

In Mexico, for example, despite the potential biases in the data, in 2005 the prevalence of depression in adult listeners was estimated at 4.5%, equivalent to 4.7 million people (Bell, Bridges, Medina and Lozano, 2005), it should be noted that this study did not include any person who is deaf in this sample.

Given these figures, it is natural to think that most of the reasons why the deaf community comes to apply for mental health services are related to depressive symptoms. However, it is difficult to assess the prevalence of depression in the general deaf population, in part, because there is more depression in the deaf community than referred to in mental health services due to the absence of the concept of mental illness in the deaf (Estrada, 2008). For example, the deaf community does not have a specific sign for the word "depression" and even there are many synonyms used as sad or discouraged, this prevents deaf people come to seek some kind of treatment.

Added to this, the lack of epidemiological research in Mexico has prevented obtaining conclusive data in regard to specific numbers. However, studying depression in this population is very important because it represents one of the side effects most commonly associated with physical disability (Rovner and Sumuely-Dilutzki, 1997).

1. Background Research of Depressive Symptoms in Deaf People

The investigation by the depressive symptoms in deaf population through assessment tools has its beginning in the late 1980s, when Leigh, Robins and Welkowitz (1988) published in the Journal of Clinical Psychology (Journal of Clinical Psychology), an article on changes in the Beck Depression Inventory

(BDI, Beck, Ward, and Mendelson, 1961) for use in the deaf community. The results of this investigation carried out in an institution of higher learning in the United States, report that between 29% and 35% of young students achieve scores between moderate and severe depression, when applying to the Beck Depression Inventory(BDI) in written form (BDI-R), adapted to deaf people. Importantly, when comparing these results with those obtained in listener population using the instrument in its original version, there is higher prevalence of depression in average levels of deaf students, but is not a significant difference when talking about levels of more severe depression (Leigh, Robins, Welkowitz and Bond, 1989).

Some years later, Marcus (1991) translates the written version of the BDI-R to video format in American Sign Language (ASL), in this case was found an average prevalence of depression (X = 14.13) among deaf students of higher education. As students whose parents were also deaf, they were those who scored lowest on the scale.

For its part, Watt and Davis (1991) used linguistically adapted version of the BDI (BDI-R) and applied it to profoundly deaf teenagers. Their results are consistent with previous studies reported, finding that deaf students had significantly higher incidence of depression (X = 10.52) and were more susceptible to boredom than their hearing peers (X = 6.59).

In 1995, McGhee made his own adaptation to the ASL of the BDI, creating a written version and a video format. Both versions were applied to a group of 48 deaf adults with similar results to those who, until then, had been reported: there are more average and moderate to severe cases of depression in deaf adults than their listeners counterparts.

Van Eldik and cols(2004) found that deaf adolescents, aged between 12 and 18, show significantly more symptoms of depression, anxiety and increased social problems that deaf children between 4 and 11 years old.

Even in geriatric samples, results have been found that are consistent with such prevalence. Werngren-Elgström, Dehlin, Iwarsson (2003) investigated Swedish prelocutive deaf, over 65 years old and users of the SL, and the results favor the profile of depressive symptoms and that even sleep disorders are more common in prelocutive deaf than in the listener population.

The new revised versions of the same instruments (Leigh and Anthony, 2001), adapted, inclusive to other languages like Spanish Sign Language (Estrada, 2008), are consistent with the results found so far, maintaining the position that there are higher levels of moderate and severe depression in Deaf people.

However, although the results suggest a higher prevalence of depression in people who are deaf, Pollard (1998) ensures that this does not mean we should expect to find depressive symptoms in each person with a hearing impairment.

2. Implications of Depression in Deaf People

Being a deaf person and suffering depression, is a twice complex situation . As we have mentioned, the people of this group do not have easy access to mental health services and these, in most cases, are not suitable for them. They do not know the concept of "depression" or "psychologist" and most of the times do not have sufficient support networks to cope with their own resources.

For these reasons, we believe that implications of depression in life of a deaf person are manifested in many areas: health, through the depressive symptoms that are normally found in deaf people, symptoms that can often be worse because the lack of proper professional care. Socially, due to the double insulation posed, first by communication barriers, and second by the depression itself, among others.

So from our perspective, the implications of depression in a deaf person can be divided into two groups:

1. The implications specific to depression, which are generalized to the entire population.
2. The implications that have only deaf people.

In the first group, we found difficulties due to the condition of depression itself; decrease in mood, loss of energy and interest, feelings of physical illness or weakness, appetite and sleep altered, in addition to other symptoms. For its part, the implications which are specific to the deaf, are due to difficulties in relationships, feelings of isolation and loneliness, and symptoms appear to have more behavioral cognitive load, probably because the manifestations of cognitive content are much more abstract than behavioral or emotional. This type of implication is closely related to self-esteem. Negative attitudes towards any type of disability are easily perceived by people who suffer. Being aware of being perceived as inferior, may adversely affect the development of self-esteem (people tend to judge themselves in relation to the external environment).

Table 1. Implications of depression among the deaf

• Less self-steem
• Increased feelings of isolation and loneliness
• More prone to boredom and disinterest
• Increased risk of suicide

Several studies support this way of perceiving the disability, for example, Gibson-Harman and Austin (1985) applied the self-concept scale of Tennessee in a written format adapted linguistically to 75 profoundly deaf and found that their self-esteem was significantly lower than reported in their hearing peers. Some other researchers have reported that people who perceived their deafness as a disability obtained lower scores on self-esteem than people who see themselves as culturally distinct (and non-disabled) (Cornell and Lyness, 2004; Crowe, 2003, Moradi and Rottenstein, 2007, Rodriguez, Maple and Sabucedo, 1997). The table below groups the main implications of depression in deaf people, especially in deep prelocutive deaf people. Rodriguez and cols(1997) studied a group of 30 prelocutive profoundly deaf social identity processes and found that prelocutive profoundly deaf young people identify with the deaf culture, perceive themselves as a distinct group (of listeners) with and unique characteristics, allowing them to have a positive self-concept. Cornell and Lyness (2004) analyzed the relationship between cultural identity and self-esteem in a group of 46 deaf college students. The results indicated that students who had a deaf identity had higher self-esteem than those who identified more with the listeners (listener identity). Similar results were reported by Moradi and Rottenstein, who, in 2007, analyzed the influence of the deaf cultural identity and the internalization of cultural standards of beauty, body care and eating disorders. A sample of 177 deaf women indicated a positive relationship between a marginal (deaf) identity and eating disorders and low self-esteem. Undoubtedly, both listeners and deaf people in general can be susceptible to low self-esteem and be afflicted by feelings of isolation, loneliness and abandonment. It is common that we feel this or find this around us. The difference is essential to consider when talking about these kind of feelings in deaf people because they probably have good reason to feel that way, because the inability to communicate with 99.72%[1] of the listener population in our country makes them feel stranger to people around them, living events, and interactions between them.

The experience of living in a world that is different is clearly reflected in the words of Bowe (1986 p.21, in McGhee, 1995), a prelocutive profoundly deaf activist for the rights of the deaf in the United States, whose parents and siblings are listeners:

> "Very soon, you say goodbye to the pride and wish to be included in the daily life of the family, your parents and relatives will speak only when necessary. There is no casual conversation, or just to relax. You can not find the little pieces that make you know the character, personality, interests and concerns of others in the talks that "talk about anything." You know your mother, your father and your sister just seeing what they do and for those occasions when they say something directly to you. Gradually your privacy increases (p.49)."

Feeling alone in a world full of people, is an emotion commonly referred by people who suffer from depression. Feeling isolated and lonely throughout life, for lack of communication with the people closest to you can increase your chances of suffering from severe depression. In most cases, at least between 90-95% (Marchesi, 1999) of deaf people live in a hearing family and can spend their entire childhood and adolescence without engaging in a conversation with someone.

Results obtained in the study of Marcus (1991), who reported that students who are deaf children of deaf parents have significantly fewer symptoms of depression than their children of hearing parents, encourage the idea that depression in deaf people is a product of isolation and rejection of the disabling condition, in that part of the population that, for whatever reason, could not accept his condition.

In fact, recent researches with deaf people demonstrate the close relationship between feeling alone and suffer symptoms of depression (Friedman, 2008). Among the greater feelings of loneliness, they more likely to have depression and vice versa.

[1] The hearing impaired population in Mexico amounted to 15.7% of the total disabled populationin 2000(the last census)(INEGI, 2000), that is 28% of the general listener population equivalent to 282, 600.

An important effect, which derives from the isolation (and a symptom of major depressive disorder) is boredom. Results of studies with the young deaf, confirm that not only raises the chance of average levels of depression, but also increases the tendency to experience boredom in many situations of daily life (Watt and Davis, 1991).

Boredom is fatigue or annoyance at having nothing to distract or entertain. It is an emotional state of dissatisfaction, in which life is perceived empty and meaningless. When this problem is present, the passage of time is very slow and pleasant experiences of life are left behind, the person feels no desire or motivation to initiate an activity (Durley, 2007). Boredom is a symptom of clinical depression, and is serious when it is present constantly for two weeks in the life of any individual.

It presented a kind of vicious circle in which the deaf are bored, for example at school, because they do not understand what their listener teacher says in Spanish, not constantly interacting with their classmates because they have not the same language. Then they begin to feel failure, isolated, bored and depressed.

Another potential implications of depression in deaf people is the abuse of substances. In this population, there is a high rate of substance abuse, one out of seven deaf people has a history of substance abuse, compared with one out of 10 in hearing people (Determ, Kordus and DeCarlo, 1999). This, as is well known, has consequences on all areas of life. The physical and mental health is deteriorating sharply, there are increased risks of contracting infections like HIV, and greater social isolation and rejection.

Discussing the implications of depression is necessary to make room for a difficult issue to treat in any population: Suicide. The highest incidence of depression in deaf people coupled with no or inadequate care in mental health treatment, obtain that in this population prevails depressive symptoms and / or deteriorates further. This suggests that the rate of attempted suicide in deaf people may be greater than in hearing people.

Vernon and Andrews (1990) compared suicide attempts among deaf students at Gallaudet University and hearing students from another school of higher learning. The results reveal that there are important similarities in the two groups, as found in the number of suicide attempts, methods used and gender of people who attempted suicide. In the archives of both institutions in a period of 20 years, were three suicide attempts a year, most of them were women and potentially toxic substances were used to commit. The only significant difference between the two groups is that, in this period of 20 years for all students who commit suicide attempts, two hearing students died from it.

In reality, there are few studies that have been undertaken to study the incidence of suicide in deaf young people. Recently, Turner, Windfuhr and Kapur (2007) reported that after an extensive literature review found only 13 articles that addressed this issue and concluded that in deaf people are present higher levels of depression and increased risk of suicide, when compared with listener population.

3. Profiles of Depression Reported in Previous Studies with Deaf People

In the literature, we found results indicating that deaf people can perceive depression differently from the listeners. These differences between the profiles of depression among deaf and hearing have been reported already in several studies (Altshuler and Abdullah, 1981; Estrada, 2008a, McGhee, 1995).

Leigh, Robins, Welkowitz and Bond (1989) conducted one of the first studies that attempted to link depression with other variables, to assess deaf population of institutions of higher education. In this research, the results indicated that depressive symptoms are associated with lower perceptions of maternal care and high levels of maternal overprotection. This, however, does not represent a significant difference between the profile of deaf and hearing depressed, since the same correlations have been reported in hearing people. What is worth mentioning is that other research as Marcus (1991) has found, there is a higher prevalence of depressive symptoms in young listeners whose parents are deaf or do not use sign language to communicate (Rose, 1996), compared with young deaf children of deaf or hearing parents who know sign language.

Given that depression is linked with feelings of neglect or maternal overprotection, and these are greater when the parents are hearing and children are deaf, it seems important to clarify that children and young deaf people (and even adults) are subjected, like any person with disabilities, to greater difficulties in interacting with their families (Guarinello, Berveian and Oliveira, 2007). On the other hand, Marschark (1993) argues that in this situation, parents tend to become more drivers, managers, overprotective and intrusive, leaving a very small chance to have a healthy social interaction.

Communication being the main problem becomes very difficult for parents of deaf children, finding a balance between care and overprotection in equilibrium, because in most cases, parents just have their own perception of the situation of the deafness , leaving aside the opinion and the feeling of the deaf child. Actually, depressive symptoms that occur in the hearing and the deaf, are often very similar, but the form and intensity in which these are experienced is what makes the difference between them. Kitson and Thacker (2000) found that in deaf people, these symptoms are characterized by agitation with hostile and aggressive feelings. On the other hand, Friedman (2008) says one of the important differences is in how they experience these symptoms; the deaf refuse to submit their symptoms to the physician or psychologist. This is largely due to a lack of mental health care. Some authors (Wermgren-Elgström and cols, 2003) reported that in a sample of prelocutive deaf geriatric assessment of subjective[2] well-being is high. In this sample, one third of deaf people have shown symptoms of depression and almost two thirds suffer from insomnia.

There was also a correlation between insomnia, depressive symptoms and lower subjective well-being. Interestingly, this study found that despite prelocutive deaf people having higher levels of depression when compared with their hearing peers, this does not imply lower perception of subjective well-being. This indicates that deaf people despite having more symptoms of depression, are not perceived less happy than hearing people. This may be because the reality of the deaf is different, all the implications that must live in a world without access to oral language, and the concept of mental illness. In the study by McGhee (1995), report indicators confirm the belief that the deaf understand, live and see the depression in a different way.

By applying two adapted versions of the Beck Depression Inventor; a written format and the other in American Sign Language through a video, three items showed statistically significant average differences: feelings of failure, dissatisfaction with oneself and sleep disorders. The same subject by answering the same question twice, with the difference that in the first time the question was in a written format and a second time the question appeared in American sign language in a video format, answering in a manner contrary.

[2] Can be defined as evaluation people do of their lives, and includes a cognitive dimension (which refers to satisfaction with life as a whole or specific areas such as marriage, work, etc..), And an affective (related with the frequency and intensity of positive and negative emotions), which through a complex interaction generated in the individual perceptions of experiences encompass a spectrum that moves from agony to ecstasy (Díaz, 2001).

Which may indicate two things: a) instruments were neither similar nor equivalent linguistic and psychological and / or b) the deaf interpret the signs differently.

For example, speaking of failure, we expect people to compare their achievements and then make judgments about the level at which they are, but in the case of deaf people, they do not know if they compare themselves with other deaf, listeners or both.

In the study carried out by Estrada (2006, 2008a) with prelocutive profoundly deaf people in Spain, the results show that deaf people reported an average score above the population recorded by the listener. It was also found, consistent with previous studies, that deaf people recorded higher intensity of depressive symptoms than the population listener. This study is the first carried out in Spain, and it was adapted linguistically the Beck Depression Inventory-II (Beck, Steer and Brown, 1996) from the version already translated into Spanish and validated in the Spanish population by Sanz, Navarro and Vázquez (2003) and translated into Spanish sign language. The final version has two formats, a video in which you have a professional interpreter in Spanish sign language and a written format where deaf people can choose their answer after seeing the question marked in the video. To distinguish it from BDI-II, our version adapted to the Mexican sign language named BDI-IIASM (ASM: ADM adapted to deaf Mexicans).

In addition to obtaining normative data reliability and validity of the BDI-II, an intervention in this study was also carried out with three cases of deaf people with depressive symptoms (Estrada and Beyebach, 2007) applying the model of brief therapy focused on solutions (de Shazer, 1985, 1988, 1991, de Shazer and Isebaert, 2003, Jackson and McKergow, 2007 Lipchik, 2002; Macdonald, 2007).

Perhaps one of the most interesting findings of this study is derived from their factor analysis, which found that deaf people often have much-motivational somatic symptoms (loss of appetite, sleep disturbances, among others), while the listener population mostly found cognitive-affective symptoms (sadness, guilt, feelings of worthlessness, etc.) according to the dimensions of depression that measures the BDI-II.

This study is apparently the first to provide data of the BDI-II factor in a sample of 114 prelocutive deep deaf people, and apparently so far no data has been reported in other studies with which they could compare the results of the factor analysis.

In discussing the differences found in depressive profile respect to gender, previous research has shown that in general population women are clinically more depressed than men (Cova, 2005). However, the results in deaf people are not conclusive. First, McGhee (1995) has reported that the incidence of depression is twice as high in deaf women as in deaf men. Sinanović, Brkic, Salihovic, Junuzovic and Mrkonjic (2004) also found evidence that deaf women have higher levels of anxiety and depression than deaf men. In the Spanish deaf community, Estrada (2008) found no significant difference between the scores of women and men, as has happened in other studies with U.S. deaf population (Leigh and et al, 2001).

The following table summarizes the main profiles of depression reported in the literature.

Table 2. Profiles of depression reported in prelocutive deaf population between 1981-2008

• Major symptoms:		
o Irritability o Agitation o Aggressiveness o Appetite changes	o Dysphoria o Somatic Complaints o Insomnia	o Substance Abuse o Disinterest in sex o Fatigue
• Major depression in deaf children of hearing parents not signers.		
• Equal levels of subjective well-being in the audience, despite higher levels of depression.		

4. Profile and Intensity of Depression in Deaf People in Mexico

In carrying out scientific research on mental health characteristics of the population, there are always some limitations, especially regarding non-observance of internal psychological processes that shape much of the construct of mental health.

Although difficulty in measuring objectively in this area can be overcome through questionnaires, auto registrations and other instruments, when it comes to evaluating the characteristics of mental health in special population, barriers are beyond what can be managed scientifically.

Speaking specifically of deaf people and the scientific study of their psychological characteristics, obstacles will not wait: How many deaf people are there in Mexico? How many previous investigations have been carried out? Where are the deaf meeting? How do I get a representative sample to make an investigation? How do I file my instrument? Who should care about my results?. These and many other questions are insurmountable barriers to be overcome if we are to make a worthy scientific contribution on this topic.

With these challenges began the adventurous task, for the first time in Mexico, to adapt to the Mexican sign language and an inventory that assesses symptoms of depression.

The Beck Depression Inventory (BDI-II, Beck, Steer and Brown, 1996) is one of the most reliable and popular among mental health professionals to identify the profile and intensity of symptoms of depression. It has also demonstrated that its reliability persists despite the different linguistic adaptations that has been subjected. For these reasons, it was chosen as a reference tool for making the experience developed in the creation of the adapted version to the Spanish Sign Language (Estrada, 2006, 2008a) to start a new adaptation, this time a Mexican sign language. The final instrument is a video of 19 minutes in length, consists of 21 items where a deaf woman points out the questions and response options, followed by a short pause in which the participant chooses her answer and the mark in the format concerned.

While the adjustment process has been long and is constantly improving, we present here preliminary results on the profile and intensity of depressive symptoms that this study has been found in Mexican deaf people.

Among the most interesting results, we mention that deaf people reported an average score above that commonly found in the general populationand that there are higher levels of depression in deaf people. In the same vein, it was found, as in previous studies (Estrada, 2006, 2008a; Leigh and et al, 1989; Marcus, 1991; McGhee, 1995, Watt and Davis, 1991) that most deaf people were placed at a level of moderate and severe depression, than those typically found in general population. These findings indicate that the intensity of depressive symptoms is higher in the deaf population than in the general population.

When talking about gender differences, no statistically significant differences were found between the results of deaf men and women, as reported in other studies (Estrada, 2006, 2008a).

According to the obtained reliability index (Cronbach alpha coefficient = 0.92,) the BDI-IIASM is shown as a reliable instrument to assess depressive symptoms in deaf persons. It should be noted that this score is above that recorded in other studies of the same nature, for example, the study of Estrada (2006, 2008) with Spanish Deaf, shows an Alpha .88 and the same value is reported in American adaptation of Leigh and Anthony (2001).

Finally, when conducting factor analysis, we found that the instrument items were grouped into two dimensions: somatic-motivational and cognitive.

The trend in research with the BDI-II (including adaptations) is reporting a general dimension that measures depression by two factors, these are reported in a fair amount of previous research in both general population (Beck, Steer and Brown, 1996; Dozois, Dobson and Ahnberg, 1998, Estrada, Landero and Gonzalez, 2009; Kojima, Furukawa, Takahashi, Kawai, Nagaya and Tokudome, 2002; Sanz, Navarro and Vázquez, 2003; Sanz, Perdigón and Vázquez, 2003; Steer and Clark, 1997; Whisman, Perez and Ramel, 2000; Steer, Ball, Ranieri and Beck, 1999) and deaf population (Estrada, 2006, 2008a). However, the finding of both factors does not assume that the profile of depressive symptoms is the same for the listener people to deaf people. By contrast, analysis of the two factors is what makes the biggest difference so far.. Deaf people in somatic-motivational dimension explains most variance to the inverse of those reported for the listener.

The only study of the BDI-II with deaf people, which included factor analysis procedure (Estrada, 2006, 2008a), reports results similar to those found in this paper: somatic-motivational dimension explains higher variance in the deaf population. These results could be interpreted as follows: deaf people in the items explained in greater suffering from depression are those that represent somatic and motivational-behavioral variables such as changes in appetite, tiredness or fatigue, loss of interest, suicide thoughts, crying, irritability, loss of energy, loss of interest in sex, among others. A limitation of the data presented in this work, and in some previous studies (Estrada, 2006, 2008a), is that the analysis have been made from cut-off points proposed by Beck, Steer and Brown (1996) for general listener population. This makes that one of the main results found so far with deaf people with regard to factor analysis is concerned, should be taken with caution because there are no proposed cutoff points for the BDI-II deaf. That is, they are more likely to find these kind of symptoms in a depressed deaf person , than variables of different nature (such as feelings of guilt and pessimism). These results leave the door open to future research that might resolve questions such as: What is the difference in the profile of depressive symptoms between the deaf and the hearing?, Will the cutoff of the BDI-II, equivalent for the deaf and the listeners?. All are determined to adapt the processes of diagnosis and psychological treatment to the needs of a community permanently marginalized.

Conclusions

Deaf people currently in Mexico represent a permanent minority in danger of being socially ignored. And as with most minorities, their fundamental rights are constantly engaged, as the opportunity to have a bilingual basic education and access to information and health services in their own language (Estrada, 2008b).

Mental health care for deaf people in Mexico is much lower than desired, lacking scientific research, diagnostic tools adapted linguistically and therapists trained in sign languages.

The only way to overcome these barriers is through the efforts of researchers and mental health professionals, who dare to make a commitment to create spaces of adequate attention to the specific needs of this population.

Evidence from the few investigations on the subject, encourage us to give greater interest to the characteristics of psychological disorders in deaf people, such as depression, which has higher trends in this population.

We are facing an almost blank canvas, where issues such as whether the assessment procedures are adequate, the cutoff points are correct, the format is optimal, language skills are sufficient, cognitive skills are consistent, among others, invite us to shape and color the map or the reliable psychological assessment in deaf people.

References

Altshuler, T., and Abdullah, S. (1981). Mental Health and the deaf adult. En L. Stein, E. Mindel, y T. Jabaley (Eds.). *Deafness and mental health.* New York: Grune y Statton.

American Psychiatric Association (2000). *Diagnostic and statistical manual of mental disorders. DSM-IV-TR.* Washington: American Psychiatric Association.

Beck, A., Ward, C.,and Mendelson, M. (1961). Beck Depression Inventory. *Archives of General Psychiatry, 4,* 561-571.

Beck, A., Rush, A., Shaw, B., Emery, G. (1983). *Terapia cognitiva de la depresión.* España: Desclée De Brouwer.

Beck, A., Steer, R., and Brown, G. (1996). *Manual for the Beck Depression Inventory-II.* San Antonio, TX: Psychological Corporation.

Belló, M., Puentes-Rosas, E., Medina Mora, M. E., and Lozano, R. (2005). Prevalencia y diagnóstico de depresión en población adulta en México. *Salud Publica Mex* (1), 47.

Connolly, C. M., Rose, J., and Austen, S. (2006). Identifying ans Assessing Depressiion in Prelocutive Deaf People: A Literature Review. *American Annals of the Deaf*, *151* (1).

Cornell, S. and Lyness, K. (2004). Therapeutic implications for Adolescent Deaf Identity and Self-Concept. *Journal of feminist family therapy: An international forum, Vol 16(3).*

Cova, F. (2005). Una perspectiva evolutiva de las diferencias de género en la presencia de trastornos depresivos. *Terapia psicológica, 23(1),* p.49-57.

Crowe, T. (2003). Examination of gender and parents´ hearing status and signing ability. *Journal of Deaf Studies and Deaf Education, 8(*2), p.199.

Cumsille, P,. and Martínez M. (1997). Síntomas de depresión en estudiantes de enseñanza media de Santiago. *Revista Chilena de Pediatría,* 68(2).

de Shazer, S. and Isebaert, L. (2003). The Bruges Model: a solution-focused approach to problem drinking. *Journal of Family Psychotherapy,* 14, 43-52.

de Shazer, S. (1985). *Keys to Solution in Brief Therapy*. New York: Norton.

de Shazer, S. (1988). *Clues*. Investigating solutions in brief therapy. New York: Norton.

de Shazer, S. (1994). *Words were originally magic*. New York: Norton.

Determan, B., Kordus, N., and DeCarlo, P. (1999). *What are deaf persons` HIV prevention needs?.* California: Center for AIDS Prevention Studies and the AIDS Research Institute.

Díaz, G. (2001). El bienestar subjetivo. Actualidad y perspectivas. *Revista Cubana de Medicina General Integral, 17(*6), p.572-9.

Dozois, D., Dobson, K., and Ahnberg, J. (1998). A psychometric evaluation of the Beck Depression Inventory-II. *Psychological Assessment, 10(2),* 83-89.

Durley, D. (27 de abril de 2007). El aburrimiento. *EMANCIPAR, 24.* Obtenido el 24 de marzo de 2009, desde http://psicopilto-monitor.blogspot.com/2007/04/la-participacin_27.html

Estrada, B. (2006). *Evaluación y Tratamiento de la sintomatología depresiva en personas Sordas profundas prelocutivas: adaptación del Inventario para la Depresión de Beck-II y aplicación de la Terapia Breve Centrada en Soluciones.* Tesis Doctoral. Universidad Pontificia de Salamanca.

Estrada, A. B y Beyebach, M. (2007). Solution-Focused Therapy with Depressed Deaf persons. *Journal of Family Psychotherapy, 18* (3) 45-63.

Estrada, B. (2008a). *Salud mental: depresión y sordera.* Monterrey, Nuevo León, México: Universidad Autónoma de Nuevo León.

Estrada, A. B. (2008b). La vulneración de los derechos humanos de las personas Sordas en México. *Revista del Centro Nacional de Derechos Humanos*, 3, (8), pp. 105-127.

Estrada, B., Beyebach, M., Delgado, C., and Freire, R. (2008). Evaluación y tratamiento de la sintomatología depresiva en personas sordas. *Psicología y Salud, 18(2).*

Estrada, B., Landero, R., González, M. (2009). Propiedades psicometricas de la versión española del inventario para la depresion de Beck BDI-II en poblacion mexicana. Manuscrito en preparación.

Friedman, J. (2008). *Predictors of depressive symptoms in persons with deafness and hearing loss.* Tesis de doctorado no publicada, Drexel University, Philadelphia, Pensilvania.

Gibson-Harman, K., and Austin, G. (1985). A revised form of the Tennessee Self Concept Scale for use with deaf and hard of hearing persons. *American Annals of the Deaf, 130,* 218-225.

Guarinello, A., Berberian, A., de Oliveira A. (2007). Deafness and attention in deaf children. *American Annals of the Deaf, 151(5),* p.449.

Hedlund, J., and Vieweg B. (1979). The Hamilton Scale for depression. *Journal or Operational Psychiatry, 10(2),* 149-165.

INEGI. (2000). XII Censo general de población y vivienda 2000.

Kitson, N. and Thacker, A. (2000). Adult Psychiatric. En P. Hindley y N. Kitson. (Eds.) *Mental health and deafness,* 337-356. Inglaterra: Whurr Publishers.

Kojima, M., Furukawa, T. A., Takahashi., H., Kawai, M., Nagaya, T., y Tokudome, S. (2002). Cross-cultural validation of the Beck Depression Inventory-II in Japan. *Psychiatric Research*, 110, 291-299.

Leigh, I., and Anthony-Tolbert, S. (2001) Reliability of the BDI-II with deaf persons. *Rehabilitation Psychology, 46(2).*

Leigh, I., Robins, C., Welkowitz, J. (1988). Modification of the Beck Depression Inventory for use with a deaf population. *Journal of Clinical Psychology, vol 44.*

Leigh, I., Robins, C., Welkowitz, J., Bond, R. (1989). Toward greater understanding of depression in deaf individuals. *American Annals of the Deaf*, 134(4).

Lipchik, E. (2002). *Beyond Technique in Solution Focused Therapy.* Guilford Press: Nueva York.

Macdonald, A. (2007). Solution-Focused Therapy: Theory, Research and Practice. SAGE.

Marchesi, A. (1999). *Psicosociología de la comunidad Sorda*. Madrid: Confederación Nacional de Sordos en España.

Marcus, A.L. (1991). The prevalence of depression among deaf college students. Tesis doctoral no publicada, Philadelphia: Temple University.

Marschark, M. (1993). The early years. *Psychological Development of Deaf Children. New* York: Oxford University Press.

McGhee, H. (1995). *An evaluation of modified written and American Sign Language versions of the Beck Depressin Inventory with the prelocutive deaf.* Tesis Doctoral no publicada. Escuela de California de profesionales en Psicología, Alameda.

Moradi, B., and Rottenstein, A. (2007). Objectification theory and deaf cultural identity attitudes: Roles in deaf women´s eating disorder symptomatology. *Journal of counseling psychology, Vol 54(2).*

Pollard, R. (1998). Psychopathology. En Marschark, M and Clarck M (Ed.) *Psychological Perspectives on Deafness* (pag. 171-197). USA:Laurence Erlbaurn Associates Publishes.

Rodríguez, L., Arce, C., and Sabucedo J. (1997). Dimensiones de identidad social en jóvenes sordos. *Anuario de Psicología, Universitat de Barcelona, Vol. 72,* pag 91-104.

Rose, N. (1996). *The relationship between coping styles and depression in a population of recovering deaf substance abusers.* Tesis de maestría no publicada. Universidad estatal de California, Long Beach, California.

Rovner, B., Shmuely-Dilutzki, Y. (1997). Sreening for Depression in Low-Vsion Elderly. *Internacional Journal of Geriatric Psychiatry, 12*, 955-959.

Ruiz, I., (2009). Intensidad y perfil de los síntomas depresivos en personas sordas profundas prelocutivas mexicanas. Tesis de licenciatura no publicada. Universidad Autonoma de Nuevo León.

Sanz, J., Navarro, M., and Vázquez, C. (2003). Adaptación española del Inventario para la depresión de Beck-II (BDI-II):1. Propiedades psicométricas en estudiantes universitarios. *Análisis y modificación de conducta, 29,* 239-288

Sinanović, O., Brkić, F., Salihović, N., Junuzović, L., and Mrkonjić, Z. (2004). Anxiety and depression in deaf and hard-of –hearing adults. *Medicinski Arhiv, 58(2),* 87-90.

Steer, R., and Clark, D. (1997). Psychometric characteristics of the Beck Depression Inventory-II with college students. *Measurement and Evaluation in Counseling and Development, 30(3),* 128-136.

Steer, R., Ball, R., Ranieri, W., and Beck, A. (1999). Dimensions of the Beck Depression Inventory-II in clinically depressed outpatients. *Journal of Clinical Psychology, 55(1),* 117-128.

Turner, O., Windfuhr, K., and Kapur, N. (2007). Suicide in deaf populations: a literature review. *Annals of General Psychiatry*, 6(26).

Van Eldik, T., Treffers, P., Veerman J., and Verhults, F. (2004). Mental health problems of deaf dutch children as indicated by parents` responses to the child behavior checklist. *American Annals of the Deaf, 148*(5).

Vázquez, C. and Jiménez, F. (2000). Compendio de escalas para la evaluación de la depresión y la manía. En A. Bulbena, G. Berrios y Fernández de Larrinoa, P. (Eds), *Medición clínica en Psiquiatría y Psicología* (pp. 288-308). Barcelona: Masson.

Vázquez, C. (1990). Trastornos del estado de ánimo (I): Aspectos clínicos. En F. Fuentenebro and C. Vázquez (Eds.). *Psicología médica, Psicopatologías y Psiquiatría. (Vol. 2)* 901-934. Madrid: McGraw Hill.

Vázquez, C., and Sanz, J. (1991). Trastornos Depresivos (I):Datos Clinicos y Modelos Teoricos. En A. Belloch, and E. Ibáñez, *Manual de Psicopatología* (Vol. 2, págs. 717-784). Valencia, España: Promolibro.

Vázquez, C., Hernangómez, L., Hervás, G., and Nieto, M. (2005). Evaluación de la Depresión. En V. Caballo, *Manual para la evaluación cognitivo-conductual de los trastornos psicopatológicos.* Pirámide.

Vernon, M. and Andrews, J. (1990). The psychology of deafness: Understanding deaf and hard of hearing people. New York: Longman.

Watt, J. and Davis, F. (1991). The prevalence of boredom proneness and depression among profoundly deaf residential school adolescents. *American Annals of the Deaf*, 136(5).

Werngren-Elgström, M., Dehlin, O., and Iwarsson, S. (2003). Aspects of quality of life in persons with pre-lingual deafness using sign language: subjective wellbing, ill-health symptoms, depression and insomnia. *Archives of Gerontology and Geriatrics, 37(1),* p13.

INDEX

A

abortion, 69, 71
abuse, vii, x, xiii, xiv, xv, 21, 22, 23, 24, 25, 26, 27, 28, 29, 30, 33, 34, 36, 37, 38, 40, 42, 45, 52, 55, 56, 59, 60, 76, 103
accuracy, 93
acquaintance, 33
adaptation, xv, 6, 21, 33, 42, 66, 77, 83, 87, 95, 99, 108
adaptations, 42, 86, 108, 109
adjustment, 108
adolescents, ix, x, 32, 97, 99, 114
adulthood, 6, 8
advantages, 11, 56
agencies, 29, 41
aggression, 8, 25, 26, 59, 85
AIDS, 63, 111
alcohol dependence, 81
ambivalence, 8
American Psychiatric Association, 110
American Psychological Association, 20
amnesia, 26
anger, 6, 9, 10, 26, 78
anxiety, 25, 26, 28, 29, 39, 78, 81, 82, 83, 90, 99, 107
anxiety disorder, 81, 82
appetite, 97, 100, 109
assault, 24
assessment, xv, 19, 43, 72, 78, 79, 81, 82, 86, 89, 93, 95, 98, 105
assessment procedures, 110
assessment tools, 98
assimilation, 59
asthma, 39
attacker, 25, 26
autism, ix
autonomy, 30, 41, 56

B

barriers, 5, 7, 32, 33, 34, 51, 55, 57, 58, 61, 74, 82, 90, 100, 107, 108, 110
battered women, xiv, 21, 22, 26, 27, 28, 29, 39, 42, 43, 44
Beck Depression Inventory, 42, 43, 46, 98, 106, 108, 110, 111, 112, 114
behavioral problems, 8
behaviors, 23, 25, 28, 39, 54, 58, 95
Beijing, 22
benchmarking, 37
bilingualism, 94
birth control, 67
blame, 26
bleeding, 38
body image, 28
bonds, 12
boredom, 99, 101, 103, 114
breathing, 43, 91, 92

brutality, 28
bureaucracy, 29

C

campaigns, 45
cancer, 71
cardiovascular disease, 91, 93
catecholamines, 78
census, 35, 36
child abuse, 23
child development, 95
childhood, 27, 37, 82, 102
chronic diseases, 88, 89
classroom, 7, 32
clients, 96
climate, 73
clinical depression, 103
close relationships, 9
cochlear implant, 10
cognitive deficit, 55
cognitive development, 79, 80
cognitive dimension, 105
cognitive function, 79
cognitive load, 100
cognitive map, 4
cognitive processing, 79
cognitive theory, 91, 93
cognitive therapy, 43
college students, 95, 101, 113, 114
color, 110
communication skills, ix, 8, 42
community, xi, xiii, xiv, xv, 1, 2, 6, 7, 8, 10, 11, 12, 13, 14, 15, 16, 17, 18, 20, 24, 29, 30, 31, 34, 38, 44, 45, 55, 57, 58, 78, 81, 82, 84, 91, 98, 99, 107, 109
competition, 16, 32, 63, 85
complaints, 22, 28, 45
complement, 65
complexity, 17
complications, 9, 39, 84
conceptualization, 10
conciliation, 41
conduct disorder, 82
conflict, 11, 15
confrontation, 85
consensus, 84
consent, 41
Constitution, 68
consulting, 31
contingency, 28
contraceptives, 71
control group, 43, 86, 91, 92
coordination, 41
coping strategies, 28, 29
coronary heart disease, 86, 93
correlation, 77, 88, 89, 105
correlations, 104
cortisol, 78
counseling, x, xi, 10, 18, 19, 20, 43, 52, 53, 113
counseling psychology, 18, 20, 113
criticism, 73
cultural differences, 15
cultural identities, 83
cultural norms, 26
culture, 3, 5, 6, 7, 10, 11, 12, 13, 15, 17, 20, 42, 44, 45, 57, 60, 76, 78, 81, 82, 85, 90, 94, 96, 101

D

damages, 39
danger, 78, 110
deaths, 38
deficiencies, 57
deficit, 83
denial, 6, 28, 37, 55
Denmark, 16, 19
dependent variable, 78
depression, vii, xiii, xv, 6, 28, 39, 42, 43, 90, 97, 98, 99, 100, 101, 102, 103, 104, 105, 106, 107, 108, 109, 110, 112, 113, 114
depressive symptoms, xi, xv, 17, 98, 99, 100, 103, 104, 105, 106, 108, 109, 112
deprivation, 19
diabetes, 39, 88, 89, 95
diagnosis, 43, 91, 109
directors, 40

disability, ix, 9, 23, 30, 31, 32, 33, 35, 36, 38, 40, 44, 45, 53, 54, 81, 98, 100, 101
disadvantages, 56
disappointment, 18
disclosure, 40, 42
discrimination, 4, 13, 23, 29, 31, 32, 33, 34, 39, 41
disorder, 16, 20, 81, 113
dispersion, 88
dissatisfaction, 103, 105
dissociation, 28
distortions, 62
diversity, 57
doctors, 6, 7, 40, 61
domestic violence, 28, 40, 41, 42, 43, 44
dominance, 24
drawing, 74
drugs, 24

E

eating disorders, 101
economic resources, 27
ecstasy, 105
educational programs, 10
educational services, 41
egg, 71
emotion, 102
emotional state, 103
empathy, 16
employment, 14, 31, 32, 35, 45, 81
empowerment, 44
enforcement, 97
England, 95
equality, 2, 13, 45
equilibrium, 105
ethics, 95
ethnic groups, 15
ethnic minority, 12, 81
etiology, 57
exercise, 91
experiences, x, 12, 14, 32, 57, 82, 103, 105
experimental design, 91
expertise, 58
exploration, 21
exposure, 42, 43, 72
external environment, 78, 85, 100

F

factor analysis, 106, 109
fallopian tubes, 71
false belief, 51, 52, 53
family environment, 30
family members, 30, 34, 39, 56, 85
family planning, 52
family studies, ix, x, xi
family support, 34
family system, 85
family therapy, 18, 111
fat, 71
fears, 51, 53, 55
feelings, 14, 25, 26, 28, 42, 53, 57, 82, 85, 100, 101, 102, 104, 105, 106, 109
fertility, 68
fetus, 69, 71
fibromyalgia, x, 39, 88, 89, 94
films, 72
financial resources, 28, 29
fitness, 79
foreign aid, 29
foundations, 93
fractures, 38
friendship, 72, 73

G

gender differences, 89, 108
gender role, 23, 24
general knowledge, 42, 80
genocide, 10
Germany, 95
gestures, 26, 65, 73
gravity, 43
grouping, 87
guessing, 61
guidance, 3, 70, 72
guidelines, 52, 55, 60
guilt, 6, 27, 42, 106, 109

H

happiness, 54
harassment, 55
health problems, 90, 114
health psychology, x, 86, 96
health services, 14, 35, 39, 40, 53, 98, 110
hearing impairment, 17, 35, 36, 51, 57, 58, 64, 65, 73, 80, 100
hearing loss, 2, 4, 5, 6, 12, 15, 16, 17, 44, 56, 57, 59, 60, 80, 96, 112
helplessness, 28
higher education, xiii, 14, 99, 104
HIV, 63, 89, 103, 111
homicide, 38
homosexuality, 58, 67
hopelessness, 28, 29, 85
host, 74
hostility, 26
human rights, 12, 33, 81, 82
husband, 35, 37, 38, 39, 63
hypersensitivity, 8

I

ideal, 53, 88
ideology, 14
idiosyncratic, 2
image, xiv, 3, 54, 62
images, 59
imitation, ix
immersion, 9
impotence, 62
impulses, 52
in utero, 71
incidence, 81, 98, 99, 103, 104, 107
independence, 32, 62
independent variable, 78
individual differences, 4
individual perception, 105
inequality, xiv, 21, 22, 31, 32
inferiority, 8
inhibition, 31, 73
inoculation, 42
insomnia, 105, 114
instinct, 52, 64
insulation, 100
integration, xi, 13, 18, 32, 53, 55, 73, 82
intellect, 15
intelligence, 16, 30, 63, 80
intelligence tests, 79
interactional perspective, 78
internal consistency, 87, 88
internalization, 101
internalizing, 39
interpersonal processes, 4
interpersonal relations, 28, 39, 52
interpersonal relationships, 28, 39, 52
intervention, 24, 42, 43, 55, 65, 66, 72, 73, 86, 90, 91, 94, 106
intervention strategies, 94
intimacy, 28, 39
inversion, 10
irritability, 97, 109
isolation, 6, 8, 9, 39, 74, 100, 101, 102, 103

J

Japan, 112
justification, 2

L

language acquisition, 79, 84
language diversity, 20
language skills, 79, 110
languages, 11, 99, 110
layoffs, 38
learned helplessness, 28, 47
learning, vii, xiii, 17, 33, 58, 60, 79, 91, 99, 103
level of education, 12, 32
loneliness, 100, 101, 102
loss of appetite, 106

M

magazines, 61

major depression, 81
major depressive disorder, 103
majority, 5, 8, 9, 32, 33, 62, 79, 81, 82, 92
majority group, 9
maltreatment, 27
management, 77, 87, 88, 89, 91, 92
manipulation, 39
marital status, 38
marriage, 27, 52, 62, 105
married women, 35
Mars, 83, 95, 104, 113
maternal care, 104
media, 7, 12, 21, 23, 52, 62, 72, 73, 77, 78, 111
mediation, 32, 41
medical care, 5, 35
membership, 3, 15, 81
memory, 18
menopause, 63
menstruation, 63, 68
mental disorder, 16, 81, 110
mental health, xi, xv, 5, 33, 45, 81, 93, 98, 100, 103, 105, 107
mental health professionals, vii, xiii, 6, 44, 82, 90, 108, 110
mental illness, 98, 105
mental retardation, 54
messages, 30, 58
methodology, x, xi, 35
Mexico, ix, x, xi, xiii, xiv, xv, 12, 14, 22, 31, 33, 35, 36, 37, 38, 42, 43, 44, 45, 53, 77, 79, 81, 82, 86, 87, 90, 94, 97, 98, 102, 107, 108, 110
Ministry of Education, xiii
minorities, 1, 4, 5, 110
minority groups, 4, 14, 26, 92
misconceptions, 55, 59
misunderstanding, 61
modern society, 62
mood disorder, 98
morbidity, 59
motivation, 28, 60, 103
mucus, 71
muscle relaxation, 91

N

national identity, 13
National Survey, 34, 35, 37, 40, 45
negative attitudes, 52, 73
negative emotions, 105
negative experiences, 14
neglect, 104
noise, 78
North America, 18
Nuevo León, xi, 46, 47, 94, 112, 113
nurses, 40
nutrition, 91

O

obstacles, 107
offenders, 44
opportunities, 14, 16, 32, 34, 38, 51, 52, 53, 57, 73, 74
oppression, 10, 11, 13
organizing, 12
outpatients, 114
ovaries, 71

P

pain, 6, 39
parenthood, 52
paternalism, 11
pathology, 83
patient care, 53
pelvic inflammatory disease, 39
perceived control, xv, 77, 89, 92
performance, 11, 53, 76
permission, 15
perpetrators, 24, 40
personal identity, 2, 3
personality factors, 4
personality traits, 2, 29
persons with disabilities, ix, 32, 36, 45, 52, 53, 55, 65, 73
pessimism, 109
phobia, 81

photographs, 67, 72
physical activity, 91
physical attractiveness, 53
physical health, 39
pleasure, 53, 54, 64
pollution, 7
poor performance, 79
positive reinforcement, 25
positive relationship, 30, 101
post-traumatic stress disorder (PTSD) 39, 42, 43, 44
pregnancy, x, 38, 39, 51, 53, 55, 61, 63, 67, 69, 70, 71
prejudice(s), 4, 30, 33, 39, 52, 55, 56, 62
preschool, x
prevention, x, 45, 86, 91, 111
probability, 39, 93
problem drinking, 111
project, xiii, 67
psychiatry, 19
psychological development, 5, 16
psychological problems, 13, 16, 97
psychological processes, 107
psychological variables, 85
psychologist, 40, 44, 100, 105
psychology, ix, x, xi, xiii, 80, 114
psychosocial stress, 84
psychosomatic, 39
puberty, 68
public health, 35
public resources, 26
public service, 5, 33, 82

Q

quality of life, 7, 10, 114
question mark, 106
questioning, 37

R

radio, 12, 14
rape, 55
reactions, 13, 59
reading, xiv, xv, 7, 31, 60, 65, 73
reality, vii, xiii, xv, 4, 5, 6, 12, 36, 38, 51, 53, 54, 55, 78, 80, 82, 83, 104, 105
recall, 18
recognition, 14, 32, 82
recommendations, 45
recreation, 91
reforms, 45
rehabilitation, ix, 24
rehabilitation program, 24
rejection, 9, 10, 102, 103
relatives, 15, 61, 102
relaxation, 42, 91, 92
reliability, 19, 87, 106, 108
repression, 28
reproduction, 53
resistance, 18
resources, 6, 27, 29, 34, 78, 100
restructuring, 42, 91
rhythm, 71

S

sadness, 18, 106
scholarship, x
schooling, 23
screening, 69, 70
segregation, 7
self esteem, 43
self-concept, 3, 84, 101
self-confidence, 27
self-control, 22
self-esteem, 13, 16, 26, 27, 30, 39, 41, 42, 84, 100, 101
self-image, 3, 31
self-knowledge, 53
self-worth, 39
senses, 78
service provider, 36
sex, 22, 31, 51, 52, 54, 55, 58, 61, 62, 63, 64, 65, 66, 67, 70, 89, 97, 107, 109
sexual abuse, 24, 31, 52, 53, 55, 56
sexual behavior, 55
sexual development, 51, 56, 61
sexual harassment, 38

sexual identity, 74
sexual violence, 23, 38
sexuality, vii, ix, x, xiii, xv, 31, 51, 52, 53, 54, 55, 56, 57, 58, 61, 63, 64, 65, 67, 70, 72, 73, 74
sexually transmitted diseases, 55, 67
sexually transmitted infections, x
shame, 30
shape, 107, 110
shelter, 2
shelters, 34, 41
shock, 6
siblings, 18, 102
side effects, 98
signs, 9, 17, 28, 84, 106
sleep disturbance, 106
smoking, 91
smoking cessation, 91
social acceptance, 12
social adjustment, 42
social attitudes, 53
social behavior, 9, 55
social circle, 33, 62
social construct, 2
social development, 5
social environment, 3, 60
social exchange, 2
social group, xiv, 1, 3, 4, 17, 33, 82
social identity, 1, 2, 3, 4, 6, 18, 101
social identity theory, 3
social network, 14, 82
social perception, 61
social phobia, 81
social problems, 99
social relations, 51, 59
social relationships, 51
social resources, 27
social services, 41
social skills, 7, 11, 84
social status, 81
social structure, 83
social support, 14, 27, 29
social workers, 42
socialization, 23
socially acceptable behavior, 24
socioeconomic status, 81
Spain, ix, x, xiv, xv, 53, 57, 58, 65, 82, 106
special education, 32, 44
specialists, 17, 34
speech, 17, 73, 79
spelling, 7
sperm, 71
spinal cord, 54, 63
spinal cord injury, 54
statistics, xiv, 21, 22, 29, 37, 38, 76, 81, 98
stereotypes, 7, 23, 29, 30, 39, 55
stereotyping, 23
stimulus, 78
stomach, 71
stressors, 80, 81
structuring, 53
subjective well-being, 105, 107
substance abuse, 103, 113
suicide, 39, 101, 103, 104, 109
suicide attempts, 103
support services, 34, 40, 42
survey, 35, 81
survival, 25, 29
survivors, 47
symptoms, xv, 17, 28, 38, 42, 43, 44, 97, 99, 100, 102, 104, 105, 106, 107, 108, 109, 114
syndrome, 28, 39

T

target population, 35
team members, 65
tension, 13, 25
therapeutic intervention, xi
therapy, 17, 42, 43, 44, 90, 106, 111
thoughts, 39, 78, 90, 92, 109
threats, 26
toxic substances, 103
traditions, 3, 14
trainees, xiii
training, x, xv, 32, 42, 45, 56, 58, 65, 91
traits, 2, 8
translation, 64, 66, 85, 87, 91, 93, 95
trauma, 38, 59, 75

U

umbilical cord, 71
United Nations, 35, 52

V

Valencia, 47, 114
validation, 18, 112
vein, 80, 108
victims, xiv, 22, 28, 30, 40, 41, 42, 43, 45, 52
video, 77, 87, 91, 99, 105, 106, 108
violence, vii, x, xiii, xiv, 21, 22, 23, 24, 25, 26, 27, 28, 29, 30, 33, 35, 36, 37, 38, 39, 40, 41, 42, 44, 45
vision, 82
vocabulary, 67
vulnerability, 30, 97

W

wages, 34, 38
waiver, 58
weakness, 100
welfare, 10, 54
witnesses, 56
workplace, 31, 32, 38
worry, 10